# The L.E. Bennett Story:
## Living the Dream

*Enjoy your New Civil Rights Experience*

*Thank you.*

*L.E. Bennett*

# The L.E. Bennett Story:
## Living the Dream

Sharon Bennett-Williams

greatunpublished.com
Title No. 365
2001

The L.E. Bennett Story:
Living the Dream

# ACKNOWLEDGEMENTS & DEDICATIONS

This book was written in loving memory of my grandparents, Anice and Daniel Bennett, without whom the Bennett family would not have been possible. They left us a rich legacy.

To my parents, Essie and L.E. Bennett, for their loving care, support, and guidance. They have always encouraged me and without ever doubting!

To my Pastors, Jasper Williams, Jr., Jasper Williams, III, and Joseph Williams of the Salem Baptist Church East, in Lithonia, GA. They have consistently fed me spiritually, encouraged me, and yielded guidance through their weekly teachings. These men of God are much admired, and a tremendous asset to the community in which they serve.

I would like to thank my many family members and friends who agreed to interviews, submitted photographs, previewed the chapters during the earlier drafts, and were always positive about this effort: L.E. and Essie Bennett, Louis E. Bennett for his wonderful artwork, James Babineaux, Thelma Bennett-Tyler, Norcie Bennett-Barnes, Martha Bennett Taylor, Hattie Bennett-Edwards, Lisa Bennett-Baskin, my children-Jerrick and Sharena Perkins, my husband-Burnett M. Williams, Susan Dixon-McClenic, Beatrice Moore-Harris, Carrie Barnes, Loretha Thompson, Doris Beckels, Donald Hollowell (famed civil rights attorney), and his wife- Louise Hollowell-retired english professor, for their words of support and encouragement. To Aunt Bernice who sent e-mails of love, Aunt Joyce, Aunt Geneva, Uncle Art Jones, Uncle Leonard, and Uncle Brother (Ollie).To all, I express my sincere love and appreciation. Thank you for all your support. Sharon Bennett-Williams

# FOREWARD

The crowd was mesmerized as they stood in front of the Alamo listening to this young man, with an east coast accent, speak on what he can do for our country. His blondish hair glistened in the sunlight and his face appeared red, from exposure to the sun. This man had a magnetism about him that caused you to like him and want to follow him. He gave off a sincere feeling about what he expected to achieve, and L.E. wanted to become part of that process. L.E. was enthralled as he stood and listened to the speech. This man was truly something to see, his speech was extremely impressive.

The crowd was caught up in the moment and the applause was thunderous. This was definitely a John F. Kennedy crowd of supporters and Kennedy was the catalyst for L.E.'s dreams. The possibility of boundless opportunities for Blacks flashed before L.E.'s eyes. There stood a white man, running for president of the United States, talking about inclusion in a country where everyone should have equal opportunity to realize their dreams. It was the first time the constitution had meaning to L.E.

# INTRODUCTION

War raged in America. The war against segregation and racism. Not only African Americans, but all people were challenged to take a stand and not allow hatred and the injustices of segregation to continue.

L.E. Bennett became impassioned when he heard J.F.K. speak in front of the Alamo, in San Antonio, Texas. J.F.K. and Lyndon B. Johnson made San Antonio one of their stops in 1960 during their cross country campaign for the presidency.

An awakening took place within L.E. like never before. He realized that as an African American, he was an American. Entitled to all the bounty this country had to offer. He could no longer go along to get along. L.E. had rights that extended past simply working only the jobs white Americans allowed him to. He was born and raised in this great country called America. He was entitled to all he could earn, and he wanted it all! However, he realized he must have a plan. L.E. would be ashamed to die, if he hadn't done something to change lives, before he left this world. His battle would be to forge integration at a major telephone company with positions other than servicemen and servicewomen (janitors & maids), for blacks.

Word of the Civil Rights Movement in Mississippi and Alabama were in the newspapers everywhere. But, the movement would need to cause a chain reaction across the South. M.L.K., J.F.K., Rev. Johns, M. Evers, and Malcolm X, were some of its famous leaders. But they weren't doing it alone. They were the catalyst that called for many others to join them in making that historic step. This was the strength of the black community. There was not just one leader, there were many. So, when one was murdered, the fight still went on. That was a misconception racists had, which is why many of the known leaders were assassinated. Oh, how wrong they were.

The L.E. Bennett story constitutes an important contribution to our history about the turbulent times during the middle fifties and sixties when the South underwent radical change.

*Amazing Grace, how sweet the sound,*
*That saved a wretch like me,*
*I once was lost, but now I'm found, was blind, but now I see*
*I was young, but I recall, singing songs was Mother's joy*
*and the shadows that would gather at the close of day,*
*as I sit on my mother's knee, in those days that use to be,*
*It was there that she taught me, all about God's amazing grace*
*Amazing grace, how sweet the sound,*
*That saved a wretch like me-e-e....*

That song. Still it brings tears to my daddy's eyes. It's been his favorite every since hearing the second verse sung by Sister Erma Webster, of the Mt. Calvary Baptist Church Choir. It reminds him of when Grandma Anice used to sing to her children. Now, I've grown up loving to hear my daddy sing "Amazing Grace." I'm grateful that we're close and we can talk about anything.

Of course, it wasn't always that way. I used to think my daddy was stern and closed-minded. Consequently, we clashed a lot. Maybe we were too much alike. That's what my mom thought, anyway. When I see him standing behind the pulpit listening to the choir, I contemplate what makes a person the way they are. He looks so calm, yet somehow distant. Often I find myself wondering what plan God has for him.

There has to be something special about the man that God calls to be his voice, proclaiming the word. Lord knows, he ran long enough before acknowledging the call. L.E. was about nine years old when he joined the Rising Star Baptist Church, where Rev. A.B. Bedford was pastor. He rose up off of the mourner's bench with tears streaming down his face. But, the call was actually first revealed to him while he was behind the house, down near the woods. He was preaching to the seamy beans, when a chilling wind gripped him and held him motionless. He saw himself standing behind a pulpit preaching to a large congregation of people, unknown to him. This frightened L.E. tremendously, and he ran back to the house and sat under the window, where Grandma kept her sewing machine. She heard him, and asked Baby if anything was wrong?

Out of breath, he answered, "No ma-a-am, I'm all right." His mother went to her grave not knowing that her baby child would one day become one of God's preachers. He could never stay away from the church house. No matter where he went, in time, he would find the nearest church. He continued to try and run from his calling. He even tried to drink it away.

"Leave me alone, he shouted. Why me O' Lord, he cried?" All of that unnecessary running from God, yet, there he is, right where the Lord wanted him. I wonder what it was like for him growing up? To understand L.E. Bennett, you'd have to understand his life and the family from which he came.

He is a very complex and studious man. He can read incessantly, and listen intently. Always looking for details. When he is doing business, he's all business; and when he engages in fun, it's all fun.

As the choir continues to sing the hymn of preparation, my mind begins to wonder back. Back to a time long past of many family reunions and stories passed down through the generations. Way back to a small town called Louise, Texas. Approximately, one hour west of Houston, off highway 59. A typical 1930's, small country town with dirt roads and farmlands, farms of cotton, dairy, sugar, hay, and beef. The town had wood framed buildings along each side of a main dirt road, some in need of repair. There you would find the grocer, a clothing store, a blacksmith, a hardware shop, etc. This was during a time when most blacks didn't own their homes or land, but rather leased from people they usually worked for. As the evening settled in, and time drifted somewhere nearing midnight, a trip would have to be made to pick up Great Aunt Martha Williams, the mid-wife, who would visit the home of Daniel and Anice Isabell Bennett. In the small country town, on December 4, 1933, at one a.m., a baby boy would be delivered. This would be the Bennett's twelfth and last child. L.E. Bennett is the name his papa decided upon. Possibly, Daniel and Anice, with their limited education ran out of names. At that time the eighth grade was as far as they could go in school. Nonetheless, that was what Daniel had given his baby son. Many have tried to change it and no one has been able to explain them, but it remains L.E. until this day. In some ways you might say he was the child of promise. The birth pangs for his arrival started at dusk, but his debut was not until the dawning of a new day. He was the baby child, and the one to whom all the attention would fall, at least for a while.

I would be remiss, if I didn't briefly tell about the siblings that came before L.E. The first born, in 1912, was Webb (Buddy). Webb is such a sweet and gentle soul. He married a lady named Eula Mae. They had three children, Isabell, Nancy, and Webb, Jr. Their son died in infancy. Webb was a farmer and raised horses. He's still residing in Louise, Texas, with Alzheimer's. All of the children and his spouse have passed.

Hattie Mae (Totah) was born in 1913. Except for her complexion, she looks the most like grandma, currently living in Dallas with one of her daughters. She married a man by the name of William Edwards (deceased), and they had fifteen children, Joyce (deceased), Raylene (deceased), Darnell, Dorothy, Annie, twins Eugene & Betty Jean, William Jr., Gale, JoAnne, Ellis, Juanita, Allen Wayne (deceased), B.T., and Ellis.

Mack was the third, born 1916, he migrated to Houston, where he met and married a beautiful woman named Ruby Holman. He passed from lung cancer and internal hemorrhaging in 1966, leaving to mourn him a young wife and seven children- Curdell, Danny, Rose, Ronnie, Enod, Maxine, & Beverly. Years later Aunt Ruby would have another son named Donald. Mack spent his last hours taking care of business, by ensuring that their home was paid for, so his children would always have a place to lay their heads.

Then came quite and mild mannered Carl in 1917. He lived out his life in San Antonio, Texas, where he married Eva Mae North, and fathered six children: Mack, Jack, Carolyn, Joyce, Brenda, and Carletta. He retired after thirty-four years with a major transportation company. He also owned land, where he raised hogs and chickens. In 1980 he succumbed to lung cancer.

The fifth child was Alzena (babygirl), born 1918. She died of pneumonia before her fifth birthday. Alzena's last words to her Mama were, "Mama take care of the baby!" She was speaking of her new baby sister, Norcie.

Next was Daniel (sonny), born 1919, who was called a blue baby. He would always have to stop and catch his breath. He'd often be seen leaning on the house and gasping for air. One day he simply took his last gasp, and fell to the ground. He was four years old when he died.

Norcie L. was seventh on the scene in 1921. She's a beautiful lady, funny, and loving. Norcie is the baby Alzena made reference to before her passing. L.E. stayed with her, during his school years, in San Antonio. She married Qunnice Barnes (deceased), who was in the army, and they had six children: Walter, Quinten, Qunnice Jr., Arrie, Marva, and Darrell. The first two boys died at the early ages of four and five.

Eighth was Martha, born 1923, also residing in San Antonio, married Ruel Taylor (deceased), and together they bore nine children: Robert (deceased), Ruel Jr., Barbara, Peggy, Herman, Elizabeth, Norman, Warren, and Audrey.

Then there was Lloyd (Blow), who arrived in 1926. He was an extremely handsome and clean cut man who, had the propensity to get mixed up with the wrong type of women as a young man. He lived with a woman considered a lady of the night, who was sent to the pen for her misdeeds. During her time of incarceration Lloyd kept company with another woman, named Cookie. One night while drinking, smoking, and partying at a San Antonio juke joint, Cookie began to make flirtatious gestures with her eyes at another rooster. Lloyd had enough and was ready to depart. He took Cookie by the hand and demanded to leave. She, in a flippant manner, yanked her hand away and shouted, No. Lloyd (Blow) grabbed her hand again commanding that they leave. Immediately, the receiver of the flirtations emerged with another acquaintance and they shot Lloyd dead. One shot went to the chest, and the other to the head, right above the brow. They were both fatal. Of course, their story was that Lloyd had a gun. However, no gun was found and there weren't any bullet holes, other than in Lloyd. The assailants were not charged with the crime. Another expendable black man.

Floyd (Honey) was born in 1928, and considered to be somewhat of a ladies man. He nearly died when he became ill with pneumonia as a child. But thanks to Grandma Anice's prayers, Dr. Bauknight, and Uncle Carl's car, who's front right wheel kept jumping off and rolling past the car, but for some reason didn't that night, Floyd was able to live a long and happy life. He spent most of his adult life in San Antonio, as well, and died from liver cancer in 1979, after two marriages and several children. One marriage was to Earline Glosson, from which two children were born. The children were Floyd, Jr., (deceased) and Virginia. There were also two children born out of wedlock, Danny and Daneille. Ms. Janie Winters was the second wife to whom Greta Legayle was born. Floyd was quite humorous, and the children enjoyed being around him. Remembering, most of all, how he would call L.E.'s house in the mornings. The oldest daughter would answer the phone:

"Hello."

"Yes, how are you doing beautiful?"

In a coy manner, she'd say, "Oh, I'm fine."

He'd retort, "Well, you're sure looking gorgeous."

Leaning on the kitchen sink, with her big pink rollers and scarf on her head she would begin to grin and shouted, "Daddy phone."

Never minding the minor fact that Uncle Honey couldn't see her through the phone. She'd snicker on back to watch T.V.

Uncle Floyd and L.E. were going many places together. L.E.

recalls a time, after getting out of the Army, when he still felt that each Friday night ought to be his night out, so, he would leave his wife and the baby at home. He'd go for a drink or two, then come back. One night, Uncle Floyd ran into L.E. at the Lincoln Ice House.

He asked, "What are you up to?"

L.E. told him, "Just having a couple of cool ones, it's my night out."

Uncle Floyd asked him, "Well, when is it your wife's night out? Since you have a night out, it just seems to me, that she is entitled to a night out, also. Don't you?"

L.E. never answered, but he sure got the message. That ended his nights out. From then on, he always took Mom, and the rest of the family with him.

Raymond (Led) arrived on the scene in 1930. Better known as the jokester. He baby talked all of his nieces and nephews, and he was extremely good at story telling. The Bennett's have this way of holding their mouth up on one side and talking in this weird, almost baby like, voice. Then we'd do this snickering type of laugh that sounded like we can't complete a word, ca-ca-ca-ca-ca. We all do it. Well, except for one cousin that has difficulty with it, Greta Legayle, Uncle Floyd's daughter. We're working on her. Cool Uncle Ray spent time in the Army before settling in San Antonio with his sweet wife Doris. They had four children, Ray, Jr., Daniel, John Lloyd, and Thelma. The third boy died at an early age, and Daniel passed in freezing weather. He was in his semi-truck, trying to take a break from the road. Uncle Ray joined the Navy and served until a medical condition forced an early retirement. Uncle Ray had two sons precede him in death before leaving this world in 1998, struck down by liver cancer.

The Bennett boys, as they were known, looked like their Father. All were six feet tall or better, wide shoulders, narrow waists, long dark eyelashes, thick dark eyebrows, nicely trimmed mustaches, and smooth brown skin. They were all good looking to the ladies, and L.E. was no exception.

Whenever people would see the boys, they would ask, "You are one of Dan Bennett's boys, aren't you?"

Their papa was Dan Bennett, a man that stood about 6 feet 4 inches. He had very board shoulders, massive muscular arms, and all the previously mentioned attributes. He was the son of John Lloyd Bennett, An African of the **Dan** tribe, born in 1829. John was taken from Liberia, Africa at the tender age of ten. His mother was fishing for the family meal along the Ivory Coast, John Lloyd (Azi Bounouku Dan) was playing on the banks. His boat trip would take him from his family of ten siblings, to Cuba, Florida, and Kentucky. He meticulously remembered the trip so he would know how to get back home. But that opportunity never came.

He was a very dark skinned man, slender, about 6'6 to 7'0 feet tall. He wore his hair in long braids down his back. It thinned and fell out as he aged, dying in 1936. In Kentucky he was purchased by the Flenard family, who later sold him to the Gray's. Grandpa John commented often on how well he liked the Gray family, and wished he was still with them. He was then sold to the Bennett's of Sandis, Texas. A town since dissolved. This is where he met and mated with Hattie Worthy, a Cherokee Indian. Said to be a beautiful woman of high cheek bones and long thick black hair, down to her hips. Dan was the only child born to this union in January 1886. There were, however, half brothers and sisters.

Dan's wife, Anice was of average height, a full figured woman, with beautiful skin, and long black hair, just past her shoulders, which she always pinned in a bun at the back of her head. Her grandfather was Austin Brown, an African-American, and her grandmother was Fannie Francis Vinson, a German woman. The daughter born to this union was Maggie Brown. Maggie married a man named Joe Parson, and their first child was Grandma Anice, born February 16, 1895.

Anice grew up to be a very industrious person. It's no wonder Anice and Dan's kids were so attractive, there was no ugly stick here. Their children were raised with plenty of love and discipline. The clan was taught to love and respect each other. If ever there was a squabble, each child would be whipped and then made to hug and kiss. This was a really bitter pill for each of them to swallow, after all, they were still mad at each other. But, the experience taught them that no matter what happened, they were never to forget that they were brothers and sisters.

Nonsense was not accepted in the Bennett household, called "The red place." An old framed four bedroom and kitchen home, with a front and back porch. The Bennett's weren't rich by any means, in fact, times were hard more so then not. But, Dan and Anice had plenty of heart for all of their children. The house was kept neat and clean. As a matter of fact, Grandma Anice had a philosophy that she acted upon daily. Everyone had to get up early each morning, and clean their room. That meant make up their bed, and sweep the floor. Then if they felt like going back to bed, they could do so. But by the time they finished doing all their chores and waited for her to approve their work, they didn't feel like going back to bed.

Grandma Anice did domestic work, attended to her family, and the home. She was a devout and stern Christian woman with little education and a lot of common sense. Grandpa Dan was a sharecropper and migrant worker with what they called the WPA. The Work Progress Administration (WPA) was a program started by the federal government during F.D. Roosevelt's administration, during the depression, which created jobs for groups of men. They were varied jobs, such as construction, digging ditches, clearing off land, cutting down trees or large branches, and hauling them off. There were even programs that involved art and building restoration.

How Daniel and Anice got together is not well known. In those days children didn't ask such questions of their parents. Records of blacks, especially poor blacks were not considered to be of the utmost importance. Much history was passed down through word of mouth. Grandpa Dan was obviously involved with someone prior to meeting Grandma Anice, but once he saw Anice he was mesmerized and fell totally in love. It seems, they married in 1911, Anice was sixteen years old and Dan was twenty-five years old. She was seventeen when she first became a mother.

L.E. started his research in 1973, and has put together a respectable family tree of descendants. Through writings and calls to various relatives, he has pieced this information together. Many friends and relatives responded with good information. However, the one thing that has troubled L.E. the most, is that he has never been able to find anyone with a photo of Grandpa Dan. It is said, that if you look at the picture of Uncle Mack or Ray, you're looking at Dan.

Anyway, Grandpa had three half brothers and three half sisters: Dennis, Chunk, Ed Holmes, Daisy, Minnie, and Liza. All were very tall. One of the brothers sticks out and leaves you with a bad taste in your mouth, but he'll remain nameless. He was considered to be a jack legged preacher, who'd often travel away to give the good word. His wife was seven months pregnant and ailing something terrible one Sunday morning. This ailment hindered her from attending services with uncle. Consequently he left her behind.

Upon his return she happily greeted him at the door, smiling "How were services dear," she asked?

Thinking she had a man in their home (which she didn't), his rebuttal was not as humane. He returned the favor by tying a rope around her legs, dragging her out the door, hoisting her up a tree, and then beating her. The family was horrified. She stayed with uncle, giving birth to a healthy child, surprisingly.

After this deed, the Bennett girls no longer wanted to call him uncle. Instead, they wanted to call him Mister. But, Anice would not tolerate any such disrespect of any elder person, even if he was a heathen in sheep's clothing. Anice's level of acceptance for disdain or abuse within her family was nonexistent. If it happened, it happened. No one and no family is prefect. She was never ashamed of any family member and their deed, and she remained proud and upright.

Grandma Anice had four sisters, Emma, Gladys, Catherine (Cat), and Fannie; and four brothers, Gilbert, Harvey, Wybranch and Cecil. Gladys had no children of her own and would shower L.E.'s children with love and gifts, especially after Grandma passed.

In the evenings, after dinner, the Bennett family would sit on the porch and Grandma would play the guitar and sing Christian songs. If anyone had forgotten to do their chores, they'd soon regret it. In those days the poor had no electricity, nor in house plumbing. If a child forgot their chores, Grandma would tell a scary story, after the singing and then before preparing for bed, she'd patiently remind them of the forgotten chores. L.E.'s chore was to empty the slop jar and bring it into the house before evening, in case anyone needed to relieve themselves during the night. Unfortunately, one night he forgot this chore. Grandma decided to tell a story about herself as a child. Her family lived in a small house in the woods, and there was a large tree that grew at an angle along by the kitchen window. One evening as the family gathered for dinner, they prayed and talked about their day.

A low growl was heard outside. As Anice looked out the window she saw a lion laying on the large bottom branch, with his front paws crossed and his head laying on his paws. The lion was peering in at them as they ate. Then Anice screamed. Her father grabbed his gun and ran the animal off.

L.E. was thinking of this story as he stood in the doorway. It was so dark, and there were all sorts of strange sounds. As this five year old stood at the door looking out into the darkness, he could hear his heart beating and feel his legs tremble. He turned to gaze sadly into his mother's eyes.

"Well, go on! The slop jar ain't gonna walk in here to ya, she'd say."

Terrified, L.E. quickly ran to the outhouse, grabbed the slop jar, and shot back into the house. He would never forget this chore again.

One day a rancid rumor reached Grandma's ears. This is one of the many stories told at Bennett family reunions, by the elder children. We'll call this woman Ms. S. for the sake of anonymity. The repugnant story was that Ms. S. and Dan had been messing around down in the woods some nights. No doubt, something Ms. S. started herself. True or not, Grandma did not want such rumors going around town about her family, ruining their reputation. Grandma marched right up that dirt road through town to handle her business. The children didn't actually witness this altercation themselves, but evidently, something did happen for the story to have continued on for years. As rumors go in small towns, it was said that Grandma Anice called Ms. S. out, to discuss the matter:

Ms. S. slithered out, and with such animosity and contempt, she stated, "What?"

It was a provocation of disrespect, that Grandma hated. She began to beat on Ms. S., and Ms. S. began wailing. When it was over, Ms. S. was on the ground. Grandma pointed her finger at the woman, and told her she'd better not ever hear of such a story again. Grandma turned and marched back down that dirt road.

As Grandpa entered the door, Grandma Anice was loading her rifle. Dan and Anice were both great hunters, and extremely good marksmen. They knew how to hit a target. They each owned a 30-30 rifle.

"So, ya think ya gonna make a fool of me, Dan?"

"Gal, what are ya talking bout. Are ya crazy?"

Anice loaded his rifle and threw it at him. Pointing her rifle at him, she stated, "I will not be disrespected Dan. Now, go for what ya know."

Grandpa dropped his rifle. "No, gal."

Grandma looked at him sternly and said, "I betta not ever hear anything like that again. True or not. Ya hear me?"

She turned, placed her rifle on the table and went to bed. The rumor was never heard of again, during her lifetime. Grandpa Dan had not betrayed Anice during their marriage, and he was remarkably good to her and the children. There were times when Grandma didn't get right up in the morning and would be sleep. Grandpa Dan didn't wake her and wouldn't allow the kids to either. He felt she needed her rest, and that's what she was going to get. Anice and Dan taught their kids and grandchildren their manner of pride, responsibility, and temperament.

L.E would later, years after Anice's death, renew contact with Uncle Melvin, his half brother. Melvin was born March 1912. One month after Uncle Webb (Buddy). His mother's name was Mrs. R. Strangely enough Melvin was welcomed at the Bennett household, as a young man. He would often come to share a meal and talk with Grandma Anice. That may had been considered strange considering the rifle incident between Annice and Dan, but she was a very open and warm hearted Christian. She and the older siblings knew of Melvin and never took anything out on him. Grandma never tried to hide anything, if that's the way it was, then that's what it was. No one was faultless and pure, and she was no martyr.

This woman, Ms. S. had two older daughters who began to pick on two of the young Bennett girls after school. Pushing on them, pulling their hair, kicking dirt on them and badgering them. Grandma was in the kitchen preparing dinner, when the girls walked in, and the girls were a sight to behold. After hearing their story, this feisty proud young mother angrily marched up that dirt road, likely leaning forward, swinging her arms, with fist balled, and kicking up dirt behind her. She probably had on one of those bright 3/4 sleeve yellow shift dresses that she made, with a white chef-like apron that had flowers embroidered on it.

Stopping in front of Ms. S.'s house, placing her hands on her hips, she called her out, again.

Ms. S. meekly came out facing Anice and uttered, "yes!"

Grandma basically stated, "Ms. S. you know I beat ya butt before, do ya want me to do it again?"

"No, Mrs. Anice, no," she responded.

Anice pointed her finger and stated, "If ya girls ever pick on my kids again, I'll be back."

She then turned and marched right back down the dirt road to complete dinner. To Anice there was no point in that type of foolishness, and she was very protective and proud of her family, she championed her kids.

My grandparents were not perfect, but they did their best to show their children the right way to live. By today's standards, they quite possibly would have been recommended for anger management classes. But, you can bet none of their children ever talked back, nor were any of them ever in jail. Daniel Bennett was a proud man and well known as a man of his word. He was the strong silent type. But when he did talk, you had better listen. He was deeply respected for keeping his word and if he said he was going to kill you tonight, you just as well get ready. He also ensured that his family was fed. One winter the food and money ran a bit low. It is said that Grandpa went to the area grocer, Mr. Ward.

"Mr. Ward, I need some things on credit, again. Now, I've always paid ya my debts, and I will again soon as I get some work in the spring. But, I got to feed my family now."

"Dan, I know you're a man of your word, but I need my money, too. I just can't wait that long for you to pay."

"Mister Ward, my word is my bond. I don't care if I go hungry, but I'm not going to let my kids starve. I need flour, sugar, & beans and I'll pay ya soon as I get some money."

"Dan, I just can't! Times are hard for everybody. If you need anything, You're gonna have to pay for it."

"I tell ya what Mister Ward, I'm gonna walk over there and get the flour, sugar, & beans; and I hope ya don't try to stop me. I'll pay ya when I can."

Grandpa got his groceries and left the store. Mister Ward never called the police, and come spring he got his money.

Dan was well known in that area. When he and his cousin first arrived in Louise, it was on horseback. They saw a wooden sign nailed to a large tree. The sign read, "Run Nigga Run, and if ya can't read, Run anyway," with a black etched stick figure of a person running. Grandpa Dan tied a rope around that sign and drug it down. The sign was never replaced. The people of this small town got along fairly well, with minimal outside influences. Grandma and Grandpa were both as protective as eagles over their children. They exemplified the type of true grit many mothers and fathers held at that time. Not just black mothers and fathers, not just American mothers & fathers, but, many mothers and fathers who took raising children with the same seriousness and zeal. However, within the family jealousy would eventually rear its ugly head.

L.E. was showered with love and attention and his sisters fussed over him, always playing with his long curly black locks. Grandpa would even bring something home everyday from work for the youngest girl (Martha), and the youngest baby (L.E.). That's what they called him, Baby, even after he was walking, talking, and running. One day while Grandma had gone into town, L.E.'s curiosity got the best of him. While the other children were playing outside, he felt compelled to climb up into the china cabinet and get a miniature souvenir "Texas Jack" knife. Grandma told him to never touch it. Which was the wrong thing to say to a kid. L.E. disobeyed, got the knife, opened it, and ran outside to show his siblings. They knew he wasn't to play with that knife. They had the look of shock and fear in their faces. So, Ray laid chase to get the knife and baby ran, holding the knife in his hand. Baby began to run across an old mattress with its springs exposed, and he tripped. As he fell to the ground, the knife went straight through his tongue. Blood was everywhere, and the baby was screaming. Norcie and Martha knew this escapade would mean sure death to them all. They kept giving him water to rinse his mouth. But, every time he'd raise the glass to his mouth the water would turn blood red. The bleeding eventually stopped. But, the ordeal wasn't over.

When Grandma returned from town and was told what happened, it was not L.E.'s tongue that had trouble. The lower part of his anatomy had a problem too. The worse thing about it was, he couldn't even cry good, because of the injury to his mouth. Ray, unfairly, was also severely chastised for making baby run.

Well, Ray soon grew tired of this double chastising and decided he'd get back at his brother by giving him a haircut. Enticing baby around the side of the house, out of the sight of the others, to play barber shop. Ray cut large plugs out of baby's head. To him this meant that Grandma would have to cut it off, and the girls would no longer swoon over L.E.'s beautiful curly black hair. On the other hand, it also meant that Ray would be at the receiving end of Grandma's wrath that day. Ray got all that was coming to him. But, L.E, still thought he could get away with anything.

"Don't you run from me, boy. Baby, get back here", Grandma shouts as L.E. ran out the house.

Everyone had a spot to sit at the dinner table. This was instituted after the older children had left home. The kitchen and eating table were all in one big room. Grandma and Grandpa each sat at opposite ends of the table. Baby's spot was next to Grandma, and he knew this. When his brother Lloyd came in for dinner, Baby was already in his brother's seat. Oh sure, Lloyd asked him to get up. But, that would be too easy. Besides, baby wanted to sit someplace different, and thought he could, if he wanted to.

"Mama, baby won't get out of my seat", Lloyd cried.

"Don't worry, I'll take care of it", she'd respond. Calmly Grandma continued to fix the plates for dinner. Then she quietly walked outside through the back door. There's one thing Grandma hated, and that's for you to run when she's going to whip you. Baby ran around the house, and Grandma behind him stroking him with a switch. As he rounded the house for the third time and received the third stroke, he could see Grandpa's strong 6'4" silhouette coming down the dirt road in the horizon. Only he can save me from this terrible whipping, thought baby. Baby dug his heels in and shot up that dirt road screaming Papa, Papa. Grandpa picked baby up, glad that he was so enthusiastic to see him. But, baby's refuge in his father's arms was but for a moment. Grandma soon appeared with a scowl on her face.

"Put him down nigga", Grandma strongly stated.

"What's the baby done Gal", Grandpa asked confusingly?

"I said, put him down Nigga, she shouted. I'm not through with him, yet."

Baby slowly felt himself being lowered to the ground. He couldn't believe Papa was going to give in, put him down, and let her whip him. Besides, Grandpa was way bigger than Grandma. L.E. was yet to learn about the woman of the house. Though he desperately tried to cling to his father's massive arms, down he went.

As they returned to the dinner table, with tears in baby's eyes and whip marks on his legs, the family quietly ate dinner. No one dared ask any questions about what happened. I'm sure Lloyd educated them on the matter, anyway. The exceptional attention paid to L.E. was over. Now, he would be disciplined just like the others.

It was January 3, 1941, when Grandpa died, just before his fifty-fifth birthday. One week before he was to go into town and take a picture with Norcie. Three weeks after carrying a large tree trunk, by himself, when his friend, Mr. Kuntz's, legs gave way on him. This left a tremendous weight on Grandpa. There was no autopsy to determine the exact cause of death. However, Dr. Bauknight believed that a blood vessel burst, and he slowly bled to death, without knowing it. The pain that he was experiencing in his chest, the night prior to his death, was a warning sign that something had gone wrong. He had risen that following morning and left for work. As usual, he kissed his wife goodbye and headed down the trail, across the creek, and took the path through the woods. That would be the same path his children would take for school, every morning. Martha, Lloyd, and Floyd found him with legs stretched across the trail and leaning back against a tree in the woods. He appeared to be sleeping, but he had entered into eternal rest. Flustered and not knowing what to do, they ran back to the house to get Norcie, who told Grandma.

Gal cleansed her husbands body as she wept and sang to him. The older children helped her to dress him in his suit. He was placed in their bed and covered with a white sheet. That evening L.E. walked into that room. He called to his father, but got no response.

He slowly approached him and whispered, "Papa are you gonna wake up?" Then with his small hands shaking, he looked at the massive form from head to toe, and pulled the sheet off his fathers face.

"Papa, I love you," he said while touching the side of his fathers face with his small hand. He began to cry and placed the sheet back over his fathers face. Funeral arrangements were made by Uncle Harvey, Grandma's brother. Uncle Harvey took his six wheeled truck into Wharton, Texas to pick up the casket. L.E. and Ray rode on the back of the truck with the casket.

The funeral was somber. A truly great man had died while on his way to work trying to earn a living for his wife and children, whom he dearly loved. Grandpa was a man among men. He was a man of his word, and always went the last mile for you. When Great Grandpa John was ill, before his passing at the age of 107, Grandpa Dan walked from Louise to Sandis every weekend to check on him and prepare food up to the very last week of his life. This was a fifteen mile trip through thick woods.

One evening on his way back from Sandis he heard soft steps behind him, as they hit the earth. He turned and saw a black panther, who then stopped and hunched close to the ground, preparing to lunge. Dan continued to walk, and so did the panther. Grandpa reached for his switch blade in his pocket. Someone was going to die tonight, and it wasn't going to be him. He stopped and wheeled on the panther again. The panther stopped and scrunched low to the ground, but didn't lunge. Dan continued his journey until he reached open space, the panther then turned and left. There was no fear in Grandpa Dan, of anyone or anything. A true rock of Gibraltar. It was going that extra mile, attempting to carry a load meant for two, that would claim his life. Even to this day, the remaining children think of Grandpa with great admiration. They knew he loved them, and he was certainly crazy about Gal; and Gal really loved "Nigga."

When Papa died the country was facing World War II. Times were becoming extremely hard for everyone, not just whites and blacks. Grandma moved from the country where she had lived the life of a sharecroppers wife, into town. She began to apply her trade as a seamstress, cook, and housekeeper for wealthier white families. She now had six of the twelve with her. Four were now married, and two had died. Words will never be able to express the brilliance of this woman with an eighth grade education, who took almost nothing in favor from others, but kept food on the table, clothes on the backs of her children, and tried her best to keep them in school. If you wanted to know how the Lord can make a way, you needed to talk to Anice Isabell Bennett. She could give you a testimony. This woman was strong to endure the loss of two small children and a husband, yet still make a way for the family.

The children never saw her cry after their father's death. They would see her suddenly excuse herself and go out to the edge of the woods behind a large tree. There she'd shed her tears with only God as a witness. She had to be strong for her family and to her that meant not letting them see her cry. She didn't become a famous person in history, but she and others like her are heroes to me. L.E. was close to both of his parents, but after Grandpa's death, his bond with his mother would strengthen.

Oftentimes, the kids would sit and reminisce of Papa and days gone by. One of the Bennett girls, recalled a time when she was about sixteen years old and they were still living in the country, and how the landowner's cows would sometimes roam over by their house. On one particular occasion, a young man came to call on one of the girls. As this young man sat on the porch, Grandpa came around from the side of the house to shoo the cows away. Grandpa looked intensely at this young man sitting on his porch. Briskly, he turned to a nearing cow, balled up his fist and punched the cow in the head. The cow collapsed to the ground and Grandpa walked off. Having seen this, the young man politely took his leave and never returned to court. The problem was that this young man took it upon himself to call on Dan's daughter, without first talking with her father. The cow was fine. It got up and went on about its business. Grandpa was indeed feared. The only person that could say or do anything they wanted, as far as Grandpa was concerned was Grandma.

Some of the older children finally had to drop out of school to help make ends meet, by picking cotton and doing other odd jobs. But through it all, the mainstay of that family's existence, rode on the back of a young mother, who never took no for an answer. She was one God-fearing woman, who was determined to see that the baby child graduated from high school. Dan and Anice did their best to raise the children in a Christian and disciplined manner, so they could survive the harsh injustices that awaited them outside of their realm. Church was mandatory, as long as you lived under her roof, even after Grandpa's death. Every Sunday would start early for

Sunday school, then church services. By this time of day it was really hot. There were no air conditioners; just the church ladies fans and that was not good enough. As Baby squirmed from sitting in that hard pew, and sweating from the heat; the church ladies would be singing and shouting thanks to God. Baby loved to hear Grandma sing, especially when she'd sit him on her knees and sing "Amazing Grace". She had a pretty contralto voice, and the Lord had blessed her to be able to use it. She sang in the choir, as well as directed the youth choir. All the children were expected to participate in services until they were of age to leave home. There were many singers in the Bennett family, as well as ministers. I'm sure that's where L.E. got his love of song.

Some Sundays, after services, dinner was served on the church grounds. Every mother brought food, and it was wonderful. The kids would play, the ladies would talk, and the men would tell tall tales.

When it came time to eat, the kids would go through the line first. They would pick foods based on who cooked it. You could hear them whispering amongst themselves.

"I don't want any of the green beans that sister so and so brought. They never really taste like green beans."

" Boy have you ever eaten any of the meat loaf that Sister Smith cooks. Man it will have you howling at the moon."

"Whew, I wonder how her family manages to take that type of cooking all week long. I bet they are sure happy when Sunday rolls around, so they can get something good to eat."

The kids laughed and played in this manner all the way through the line, and it was all in good fun. There was no such thing as lunch. You got breakfast at home, church all day, then dinner on the church grounds.

Like an eagle, Dan and Anice guarded over their young; and the Bennett children deeply loved their parents, even in death. My daddy is a very gifted and talented man, blessed by God to be able to do so many things, well. Of course, I could just be a little prejudice. He has written many songs and poems. He once had a song he titled, "A Time and Again" that he copyrighted, in the mid sixties. It was his love song for Twinkie, my mother. He distributed this song to various artists, like Nat King Cole and Frank Sinatra, just to name a few. He later heard a song with profoundly similar lyrics sung by Frank. He felt confident it was his song, but the song never caught on, so he never gave the matter further thought. He always reminisced, if it had been sung correctly, then maybe it would have done better. He had this brown duffle bag full of poems and songs, which were left in the attic of our first home. The new owners disposed of it, before L.E. could get back to reclaim it. He's never had the burning inspiration to start again. Another talent he possesses is the ability to take the complicated, and make it simple. If there is a way to make a difficult problem more tolerable and understanding, give it to L.E.; he'll find a way to reduce it to a simple form and get maximum results.

## <u>WHEN I WAS YOUNG</u>

Well, when I was a young one
Growing up long, tall, and thin
I would reminisce on
Momma's guiding hand.
She walked, talked, and prayed with me
So my soul would not be lost,
To her I owe it all, I can never pay the cost.
She's the gleam in my eyes,
And the light in my heart.
To you dear Lord I pray, please,
That we should never part!

**SHARON BENNETT-WILLIAMS (10/00)**

# CHAPTER II

O h no! He's going to shoot me," L.E. shouted as he jumped out of his seat running toward the exit. A large tent had been erected in a field close to town in Louise. A Cowboy and Indian movie was being shown. People of all ethnic backgrounds came out, mostly the poor, to see a movie. The nearest theater was ten miles away in El Campo, and if you didn't have a car, you didn't go to the movies. The kids sat in the front rows Black, White, and Latino. The mothers sat towards the back. Thank goodness Grandma Anice was sitting by the aisle, so she could grab L.E. as he ran by. Hugging and kissing him she gently explained that the larger than life cowboy who rode up on his horse wasn't really pointing his gun at him. It was only make believe. L.E. watched the rest of the film from his mother's lap. This would not be his last horrid movie experience.

When Grandpa died, L.E. had just turned eight and started school in the fall. Almost, a year later than usual because of his December birth date. He would prove to be an exceptional student. But, the distance to walk to school was really too far for a child of that size. No buses were provided for African-American children. They walked, while others rode. The white children on the big yellow buses taunted him as they rode by. Angrily, L.E. picked up rocks and threw them toward the bus, never actually hitting it. It was just a way of letting off frustration. The other siblings had to drop out of school to help Anice make ends meet. They worked various odd jobs from cleaning houses to picking cotton. L.E. was not yet old enough to pick cotton, but he would often ride on his sister Norcie's cotton sack. It was a wonder that she didn't make him get off. Perhaps, she knew that when a worm fell on the sack, he would shriek and run back to the turn-row. Daddy has never liked worms, and still doesn't until this day.

Many families would make considerable money picking cotton. Though this would not prove to be L.E.'s forte. Besides, Anice had other plans for her youngest son, that was for him to finish school. Since the others had to help by working, the mantel for a full education fell on him. L.E. would attend the third through fifth grade in El Campo, Texas. Norcie would then take him to San Antonio, TX to live with her for the sixth through the ninth grades. However, they wouldn't enroll him until he had a real name. To them L.E. was unacceptable, and not a real name. So, she gave him the name Lee Ernest. For L.E., school was a fertile field. He could never get enough of the classroom experience. There was always an overriding mission in him, other than wanting to learn. An education helped him to achieve more, and he wanted desperately to do something to help bring some joy into his mother's life. In his eyes, she was a beautiful, brilliant woman who labored hard to provide for her children, although she bore the heartache of a deceased spouse and two dead children. It meant everything for at least one of her children to graduate high school. Anice worked tirelessly during L.E.'s junior and senior years to make certain he had everything the other children had. So much so that her little feet were swollen. She wanted him to be able to sit in that auditorium with his head held high, and hers would be up as high as the other parents.

To help, L.E. worked various summer jobs. He first tried picking cotton for two weeks. He even picked 205 pounds in one day. But he still wasn't very good at it, so, he sought other work opportunities. He then went to Houston to stay with his brother, Mack. There he obtained a job as a busboy at a local restaurant. The ad in the paper asked for busboys, stating they'd be paid salary and tips. So, when cleaning the tables L.E. and the other busboys would take the tips. This, of course, became a problem, because the waitresses were suppose to get the tips. L.E. organized the workers and a meeting was held that evening with the manager.

Basically, L.E. told him the ad was false advertisement to entice workers. The manager said the waitresses are to collect the tips and split them with their busboys. There's no way to guarantee how much was actually collected from the table, or that the waitresses would split them. Not everyone wanted to take a stand and boycott or quit, if needed. L.E. felt disenchanted with his first failed attempt at negotiation through communication and quit that job. A few others stated they wouldn't return either.

L.E. then secured employment in San Antonio at, Sommers Drugstore as a short order cook and busboy. This would become his regular summer job, that enabled him to buy clothes and other items a young man needed. San Antonio was always considered a premier city by L.E. There is something about the flavor of San Antonio. Her people, her climate, her ethnic makeup. It just all seemed to say "we are family." Yes, we are different in our own way, but there's pride in saying, "I am a San Antonian." But despite how beautiful and wonderful a place San Antonio is to live, it still did not escape racial prejudice. It hung around like a dark cloud.

One Saturday afternoon L.E. decided to go to the movies at the State Theater. It was located in the Stowers Furniture building, on the corner of Main and East Houston, in downtown San Antonio. The "colored section" of the theater was located upstairs on the third floor balconies. L.E., eating a Hearshey's candy bar, got choked, and began to cough. There were no rest rooms or fountain facilities in the "colored section." So, he had to walk those stairs all the way down to the first floor. Gagging and trying desperately to dislodge that chunk of candy and get air into his lungs. Though he was getting dizzy and feared he might die, he didn't panic. If he could just make it to the fountain, a drink of water would help to dislodge that chunk of candy from his throat. As a teen, that angered him. He finally made it to the fountain, sipping, gagging, and coughing, the hunk was dislodged. He wet his handkerchief and wiped his face. Why did he have to travel such a distance for the simple element of water, to avoid choking to death. A decision was made that very day not to ever go to another theater that compromised his safety. It was this incident that made him so keenly aware of being treated differently. Sure, the lunch counter at Sommers was segregated, and blacks had to get their food to go. But, no mistreatment was experienced or observed. It was considered business as normal. However, now he became painfully aware of the consequences of racism. A person should never allow themselves to be subjected to the poor treatment of segregation for the sake of attending some entertainment event. Many individuals have been subjected to bad situations in order to earn a living for their family. One has to have a place to live and food to eat, it's true. But, it really isn't acceptable in the workplace or on the street. What's even worse is to allow yourself to be treated in an offensive manner, and you are spending your hard earned money. The ticket prices were no cheaper for the inconvenience of the "colored section." For someone to treat you like you're less than human and make you pay for the privilege, is utterly ridiculous.

After the movies incident, L.E. hopped the bus home. Another black gentleman who'd also boarded the bus, sat about midway. At the next stop a white gentleman got on the bus, and all the seats were filled. He told that black gentleman to get up and give him that seat. The response was, "Go to hell." The white gentleman's face became flushed and he was furious. A fight ensued between the two and the black gentleman pulled a knife. Thank goodness others interceded and stopped the fight. The black gentleman maintained his seat. Considering these occurrences, L.E. figured it would be best to finish his sophomore through senior years in El Campo, near his mother. The summer activities were about all he could stomach.

As far as affairs of the heart go, L.E. had his share. The first was a girl by the name of Zara. L.E. was about twelve years old, and Ms. Zara was one grade level ahead of him. They would pass notes to each other through a mutual friend by the name of Ernestine Boston. They kept her busy passing notes from Ms. "Short" Anderson's homeroom, to Ms. "Tall" Anderson's class. The teachers were nick named this way because Ms. "Tall" Anderson was just that, very tall. Ms. "Short" Anderson was very short by comparison. So, as L.E. sat at his desk, Ernestine passed the note. He read it and stuck it in his desk. Ms. "Short" Anderson saw him and asked did he just put a note in his desk?

L.E., said "No, Mame." She then asked another student, next to him, if he saw L.E. put a note in his desk?

Ceasar said, "Yes, Mame."

Ms. "Short" Anderson then asked L.E. to read the note out loud. Which he did. This somewhat curtailed the note sending. He would have a number of girlfriends through the years, whose fathers would object to any type of courting. L.E. was very cute and still had thick wavy hair. He thought he could date any girl he wanted to. On one occasion he and some friends attended a girls basketball game at E.A. Greer High School. He was wearing his blue and gold letter jacket, so there would be no misunderstanding about who he was. He saw a cute light skinned young junior that played center by the name of Essie L. Jones. After the game he decided to approach her for a date; he was popular, suave, and no one had rejected him, yet. He shot her a lame line and asked this particular young lady to go out? She told him to get lost, turned her back to him and left. So much for suave.

Alma Charleston was a classmate, and the object of L.E.'s romantic interest, during his freshman year. Alma, as many before her, tried to teach L.E. how to play the piano. But, he wasn't interested in music beyond the point of trying to sing. He was, however, a popular athlete participating in basketball and football. He even helped develop most of the plays for his team. While Coach McIntosh was a wonderful person, he knew very little about the games. He didn't even know the proper way to wear the protective pads. Coach, a general studies teacher, not an athlete, was grateful for the assistance. Alma had a baby-sitting job after school for a white family. One day, in order to spend more time with Alma, L.E. decided to walk her to her job. Alma's father didn't allow her to date yet, so L.E. would wait up in Ox Blood. This was a little section of town where black folks congregated for fun times. Many of the juke joints were located in Ox Blood. While walking through the white neighborhood, a woman deliberately came to the front door with her German shepherd. Opening the door, she sic'ed the dog on Alma and L.E.. Seeing the dog approach growling and barking, Alma started to run. But, L.E. grabbed her and said no-stand still. He remembered his mother telling him to never run from a dog. It'll tear you in pieces. Holding firm and facing that German shepherd, the dog stopped. Finally, seeing that they had refused to run, the woman called her dog back.

Life will never be at its best in America, until we can meet each other on a level playing field, and treat each other as fellow travelers. I can't help but to wonder what manner of delusion it is in a person's head that makes them think they're better than another. What makes some people think they have the right to rule or have dominion over another. To exact persecution and sadistic injury upon another, in the name of what they dare call some form of Christian righteousness, is the lowest form of human behavior.

Finally, graduation day would come for the E.A. Greer class of 1953. Grandma Anice and L.E. had worked hard to help make it happen. He would not only graduate, but he was chosen class Valedictorian. Oh, he was a sharp looking graduate. With a black suit, white shirt with French cuffs, and black shiny shoes. Anice was so proud, she could have burst. The nights events were all planned, and the students had looked forward to this all year. L.E. was to be the soloist, as well. The love song was called, "The Other Side of Mountain," by Arthur Prysock. The lyrics went something like this:

There was a boy, there was a girl, and if they had met.

They might of known a world of joy, but he lived on the other side of the mountain And she lived on the twilight side of the hill.

They never met, and they never kissed and they will never know the happiness they missed, For he lived on the other side of the mountain and she lived on the Twilight side of the hill. A beautiful song, and tale of love. Well, L.E. has this  Billy Eckstine type of baritone voice, and it promised to be a special treat. He could really croon with that sweet voice, that gave all the girls goose bumps. He had worked really hard for this day, with the music teacher, Mrs. Baker.

There's always a teacher from high school that makes all the boys crazy, or all the girls go ga-ga. Well, Mrs. Baker was one of those. A very beautiful, young brown skinned woman, who just made the boys heart go pitter patter, when she walked by. It was her job to rehearse L.E. for graduation night. Everyone was looking forward to it, because they'd heard the rehearsals and commented on how good he'd sound. Everything was going beautifully, the momentum was building, and anticipation was running wild. This wonderful baritone voice would finally be heard by all. The curtains would open and L.E. would be seen standing center stage, sharp as a tack and sounding like Prysock and Eckstein. Mrs. Baker hit the key, the lights spotted on L.E., but when he opened his mouth to croon that lovely song, something came out that he'd never heard before. His voice was beyond tenor, and baritone was no where to be found. It was more like the cry of a Banshee. It was a complete disaster. He never thought he'd get so nervous. But, somehow he managed to survive the embarrassment, to complete the song. Scratching and screeching all the way. His friends almost laughed themselves to death. Even with this flop, at such a pivotal moment, the evening and his high school years were still an honor he cherished. After all he was the Valedictorian of his class, the high school quarterback and an exceptional basketball player. He wore his blue and gold letter jacket with pride.

With honors L.E. Bennett, valedictorian of the class of 1953, the announcer said, as L.E. strolled across the stage for the first diploma in the Bennett family. Anice Bennett was one proud woman that eventful day. With swollen feet and circles under her eyes, she cried tears of joy. When L.E. received his diploma, it wasn't just for him, but for his parents and for all his brothers and sisters. Grandma pulled the rabbit out of the hat again.

We just know that Grandpa, Dan Bennett, was looking down

on them saying, "Gal, you did it again. I knew you would." Anice was one unique and wonderful person, who always just seemed to have all of the answers to life's most difficult problems. She gave so much of herself for the well being of her children. Maybe this book should have been written about her. When I think of how hard she worked for her children, I think of this verse:

## ECCLESIASTES 3:1-8

TO EVERYTHING THERE IS A SEASON, AND A TIME TO EVERY PURPOSE UNDER HEAVEN;

A TIME TO BE BORN, AND A TIME TO DIE; A TIME TO PLANT, AND A TIME TO PLUCK UP THAT WHICH IS PLANTED;

A TIME TO KILL, AND A TIME TO HEAL; A TIME TO BREAK DOWN, AND A TIME TO BUILD UP;

A TIME TO CAST AWAY STONES, AND A TIME TO GATHER STONES TOGETHER; A TIME TO EMBRACE, AND A TIME TO REFRAIN FROM EMBRACING;

A TIME GET, AND A TIME TO LOSE, A TIME TO KEEP, AND A TIME TO CAST AWAY;

A TIME TO REND, AND A TIME TO SEW; A TIME TO KEEP SILENCE, AND A TIME TO SPEAK;

A TIME TO LOVE, AND A TIME TO HATE; A TIME OF WAR, AND A TIME OF PEACE.

# CHAPTER III

He's in the Army, now! It was the summer of 1953 and the country was still involved in the Korean war, which had begun June 1950 after the invasion of North Korea into South Korea. The military was taking plenty of young men to replenish their troops. Once again Black Americans would fight in a war for their country. While most Americans fought one war, African Americans had two-the one aboard and the one at home. L.E. had registered, as required by law, after his 18th birthday. He was sent to Houston, Texas for testing and his examination. Things went off without a hitch. L.E. was feeling pretty grown up and proud that he'd be able to help his mother financially, as she'd done for him all those years. Now it was his turn to give back and he looked forward to seeing other parts of the world, besides Texas countryside. There were eighty-four other young Americans, of varying ethnicity, waiting to be tested. Of all those examined, four young men would score high enough to be considered for Officer Candidate School (OCS). Three were white and one was black, and his name was L.E. Bennett. However, L.E. elected not to pursue OCS, and was shipped immediately to Fort Sam Houston Army Base in San Antonio, Texas. After the traditional indoctrination, transportation to Camp Roberts, in the San Joaquin Valley of California, would be the next step. There he would spend sixteen weeks in basic training, where again he would be approached about considering OCS. Again he elected not to accept the opportunity.

When L.E. looks back on it, he considers that decision to have been a mistake, but just one of the many he would make in life. Even today, he's still not sure why he refused the opportunity. He does recall the rumors going around, that a Second Lieutenant's life was not worth a plug nickel in Korea. That is where he was destined to go, and possibly where his life would end, if he took a position of leadership. Also, that type of strict regimentation wasn't for him.

Their commanding officer for basic training was First Lieutenant Huber. He was a tall drink of water and he could really march the young soldiers. They would head out in the early mornings after reveille and breakfast, across the parade field, which was about a mile long, and a quarter mile wide. One soon discovered that keeping up with Lt. Huber was a full days work. Man, could that white boy march. L.E. was elected as the Guide-On Bearer for his company, and that meant he was right up front behind that long legged yahoo of a commander. Lt. Huber was exemplary, for which he was admired. L.E.'s stay at Camp Roberts was pleasant, and for the most part, everyone got along. There was, however, one incident of racial confrontation. A black trainee by the name of Conners would always hide under his bunk after breakfast to catch a quick nap. Another trainee by the name of Anderson, a young white boy with red hair and freckles, saw this as lazy. He decided to get a group of other white soldiers together and teach Conners a lesson. Even though barracks were integrated, Anderson didn't reside in Conners' barracks. Somehow, the word got out, because a trainee called Billy Beck came to L.E.'s bunk that night to alert him of the plan. L.E. then told Beck to alert the other black soldiers.

When Anderson and his gang came to the barracks he stated, "Conners, we're going to whip your ass."

L.E. stood in the aisle facing Anderson and rebutted, "Anderson, if you want Conners, here he is, but nobody else had better lay a hand on him. It will just be the two of you slugging it out."

Anderson said, "We don't have anything against anybody else, we just want lazy Conners."

L.E., again told him it will just be the two of them, or all of them. Anderson and his friends hem hawed around for a while, and then the crowd dispersed, and everyone went to sleep. That has sort of been L.E.'s life, standing up for the under dog. The first fight he had in elementary school, was because he took up for a boy who'd gotten a bloody nose. L.E. had to give that bully a bloody nose, too. There were a lot of other individual scuffles in camp, but never did another such group incident occur.

The young men would complete their basic training, get two weeks leave, and then report to Camp Stoneman in California. Here they would prepare for the long grueling trip overseas, with stops in Honolulu, Guam, and Japan. The stay in Tokyo, Japan would be one month at Fort Clark. In Tokyo there were days, for just a short period, that even the mere thought of food made L.E. feel like throwing up. But, after finally becoming acclimated to the environment, the people and the place, his appetite slowly came back. He began by eating small amounts of the foods in the mess hall, and pretty soon he was back to normal. They would then ship out to Yokohama, Japan and from there to Pusan, South Korea and from there by train to Yongdongpo, Korea. The soldiers were picked up in two and a half ton trucks and taken to the 45th Engineering M&S Company where they would be interviewed and given assignments.

L.E. was interviewed by a Major Somers, who asked him if he knew how to type? The reply was no. Major. Somers stated that someone with his educational background, should take typing and if he did, it was highly possible that he could become the company clerk with a rank of Sergeant First Class by the time he returned to the states. The major told him to go over to Second Army and enroll in the typing course, upon completion, return the notice and he'll see about having L.E. work in his office. In the meantime, L.E. was assigned as a motor vehicle dispatcher, which is a clerical type job, and he mastered it in no time. He would work a twenty-four hour shift and be off for forty-eight hours. He could use the off time for typing class. Chief Warrant Officer Duffy and Sergeant 1st

Class Grant ran the motor pool. These two were wonderful people to work for.

They were strict about orders given, but their attitudes were such that it made you feel good about following those orders. Consequently, L.E. enjoyed his work at the motor pool and would always find any excuse not to enroll in typing classes. Thinking back, he believes the reason he didn't follow up with typing class was the same reason he didn't go to OCS. He didn't like the idea of such a stern regimentation. Your every step was dictated. What you wore, what you ate, where you slept, when to go to bed, when to get up. One became more like a clone. If he completed classes and made Sergeant First Class, he might become weak enough to re-enlist. Military life in reality just wasn't for him. He did his job well as a motor vehicle dispatcher and was well on his way to becoming a sergeant, when he got crossed up with a Captain who thought L.E. and he were seeing the same woman. Of course, L.E. wasn't but that didn't matter because the Captain already believed otherwise. When promotions came down, he was denied.

The First Sergeant came to the motor pool and explained the reason to L.E. He didn't know if the reason for his denial was true or not, but he never confronted the Captain about it. He simply told the Sergeant the Captain was barking up the wrong tree, and that he had nothing to do with Ms. Kim. He had very little time left in Korea, so that was the least of his worries.

One night when the Officers were having a party in the B.O.Q., Colonel Kibler, commander of the 45th Engineering, had requested that Cpl. Worley go to 8th Army Headquarters in Seoul and pick up some of his friends. Prior to this occasion Col. Kibler had written a directive that stated, no motor vehicle was to go out after eighteen hundred hours without an authorized permission slip, signed by him. The Colonel got wind of unauthorized vehicle usage and he was determined to put a stop to it. It was after midnight and L.E. was on duty. He had already prepared for bed, striped down to his skivvies, and in his cot, when there was a knock on the door.

He told the visitor to come on in and turn on the light. When the light came on, in the door stood Col. Kibler, their commanding officer. He had a Major General, a Brigadier General and another full Colonel with him.

Kibler had this big smile on his face. "Hi, Corporal Bennett. I would like to get my vehicle, so I can take my friends back to 8th Army Headquarters in Seoul. I will also need one of your drivers."

Still in his cot, looking back over his head at the Colonel, politely L.E. said, "Yes sir, if you would just sign an authorization slip, I'll have a driver take care of you." The next voice L.E. heard thundered like a 105 Howitzer had fired, and almost shattered his ear drum.

"Get out of that cot, and get my vehicle."

He jumped out of the nice and warm cot, and stood in his skivvies.

"Stand at attention Corporal," Col. Kibler stated.

Looking directly at Col. Kibler L.E. said, "Sir, you have a directive that says no vehicle can leave this motor pool unless an authorization is first signed by you."

The Col. Looked at him and asked, "Where in the hell is the damn authorization slip." He signed it and he was off to Seoul.

The next morning, before getting off duty, Officer Duffy came by the motor pool.

"Well, L.E. looks like you had some company last night, and things got a little hot and sticky around here", said Officer Duffy. Duffy also said that Col. Kibler asked him to commend L.E. for sticking to his guns, because he now knows that if L.E. had the Colonel sign an authorization from, then he was surely making everyone else complete a form.

Officer Duffy told L.E. "Just between us, the next time Col. Kibler came over in the middle of the night for a vehicle, to give him the whole damn motor pool, if he wanted it, damn it."

L.E. said that he most certainly would, and they both laughed about it. However, every time thereafter Col. Kibler had his driver pick up a requisition slip and return it signed, if he wanted his vehicle after 1800 hours.

Col. Kibler was a true gentleman, and his presence commanded everyone's respect. The whole company was saddened when he received his orders to go back to the states.

It was a hot summer evening, and L.E. was sitting outside the Dispatch Office when Private Pace paid him a visit. Pace had been asked by Sergeant 1st Class (SFC) Grant to go up north to the Demilitarized zone, and pick up a jeep that had been loaned out. L.E. had never been up north, so naturally he was interested and excited to make the trip with Pace. They left the next morning. The scenery was beautiful. It was a part of Korea that he'd never seen, so he just sat back and enjoyed while Pace drove. They left Yongdongpo around noon and arrived at the Demilitarized zone (DMZ) in the early evening. They were greeted by the Motor Sergeant, who made them feel welcome and at home. There were no intentions to spend the night. They enjoyed the fellowship, which included a few cold ones, and then decided to head back to Yongdongpo, South Korea. Pace was driving the lead jeep with L.E. following close by. It was mountainous terrain, and they drove carefully, because of the loose gravel on the winding roads. Occasionally, while going around a curve L.E. would be out of Pace's view. As they proceeded down the mountain, L.E. hit some loose gravel and went off the road, with only part of the jeep still hanging on the side of that mountain. Afraid to move, for fear the jeep would go completely over the edge and tumble down the mountain side, he sat motionless. His only hope was that Pace would realize he was no longer following him, and turn around. Talk about living on Mama's prayers.

As he sat there waiting for Pace, his mind raced back to basic training at Camp Roberts, California, when they assisted fighting a forest fire in the San Joaquin Valley. While on a rest break from fire fighting the men decided to hike up to the top of a mountain and take a look around. While watching the fire in progress, and enjoying the beautiful untouched scenery, L.E. moved about and his foot hit some loose dirt; he began to slide down the side of that mountain. Reaching out to catch hold of anything, he grabbed a small tree that was growing up the side of the mountain. It broke his slide. After regaining his footing, he looked down at that small plant which still showed his hand grip. It grew in loose dirt, and it came right out when he yanked on it with his hand. His life literally flashed before him as he thought how his mama's prayers and the grace of God kept him from going off the side of that mountain. There was no way a little twig like that could have broken the slide of a 6'1", 195 pound man. It was the hand of God, and mama's prayers. About 500 feet or so below where he would have fallen, were jagged rocks where his body would have landed. If he had fallen, he would possibly have lost his life.

Now, here he was again on the side of another mountain, with his life hanging in the balance. He felt he was living on his mother's prayers, because his prayer life had stopped once he left home. He sat as still as possible, waiting on Pace to come back, and he began to pray.

Soon he saw lights coming back up the mountain; sure enough it was Pace. L. E. rejoiced to see him.

Pace stopped his jeep, and rushed over shouting, "For goodness sakes, don't move. Keep still, I'll take my chain and carefully hook onto you. I'll drag you back toward the center of the road."

Finally, Mr. Pace had L.E. hooked up, dragging him until L.E. was able to get traction. He was not as prayerful as he is now, but thank God he had a praying mother. Grandma Anice had told L.E. that she couldn't go with him to Korea, but she knew someone who would, and she would leave her baby in His hands. Thank God for Grandma's prayers. Pace and L.E. would stay in real close proximity to each other all the way back to Yongdongpo. They arrived very late that night, and spent a good deal of the next day in the bunk. It had been a good trip, but it was nice to be back in camp safe and sound. He would never forget Pace's friendship, and his heroic efforts to save a life. They've lost contact, but every so often he has fond memories of this friend in deed, in his time of need.

The First Sergeant Savage tried to get L.E. to re-enlist, stating that he'd ensure he wouldn't be denied a promotion again. But, L.E.'s eyes were on the states and seeing his family again. He had enough of military adventures.

**GENESIS 28:15**

And, behold, I am with thee,
and will keep thee in all places
Whither thou goest,
and will bring thee again into this land;
For I will not leave thee, until I have done that
Which I have spoken to thee of.

# CHAPTER IV

Once L.E. arrived in El Campo for leave it was good to see his mother again. Grandma Anice looked well. They stayed up most of the night talking about the happenings around El Campo. She also wanted to know how her son liked the Army. L.E. assured her that his discharge of June 1956 couldn't roll around quick enough for him. Military life had its benefits for many, but it just wasn't for him. The next few days were spent visiting old friends, and, of course, Anice had to show off her tall, healthy, handsome son to her friends.

Revival, which was held in the school house, had been going on all week at his home church, Mount Olive Baptist Church. Pastor A.A. Hargrove was hosting, with the Rev. B.F. Langham of the Mt. Calvary Baptist church of San Antonio, Texas. It was a Friday night and L.E. felt compelled to go to church. Ordinarily, he would have stayed up in the West End (Ox Blood) with the fellows, as he had done every night that week. His mother had been attending services without him. She sang in the choir with her beautiful contralto voice. Anice also directed the children's choir. L.E. knew she would be happy to see him attend.

L.E. headed for a seat on the left-hand side of the main aisle, facing the pulpit. The church was full. After a while when he noticed a young lady standing in the choir, by the door ushering. It was Essie Lee Jones, the girl he had tried to ask for a date after one of her basketball games. She'd told him to get lost. Looking at her, he noticed a bright yellow aura around her. L.E. thought to himself, this girl has grown into a really beautiful woman. Maybe he should try talking to her again. After all, time had passed, and he wasn't the playboy he once was. Possibly, if he used the right approach this time, she'll at least give him the time of day. L.E. wasn't seeing anyone at the time, and all his former girlfriends were either gone or married. What did he have to lose? He watched her throughout the service. She didn't appear to notice him in the congregation. She stayed busy doing what ushers usually do, manning their post.

Patiently waiting for the end of service and benediction, his mind began to wonder back to all those many revivals he and his siblings had attended with their parents. Specifically, his brother Carl. It seemed that every revival, Carl would answer the call to discipleship and go sit on the mourners bench. Carl would accept Christ and then be baptized. On this one particular revival night Carl was already agitated. He'd been gathering a collection of catalog ordered shirts with matching ties. While getting dressed for revival he'd noticed some of his ties were missing. Anice and Dan didn't want to hear any mess or arguments that night about ties. They had to simply get dressed and get to church. As soon as Carl arrived on the church grounds he saw his sisters Norcie and Martha talking to two young boys: darn if those boys weren't wearing his ties. Carl marched up to them and yanked the ties off their necks.

He said, "What are you little niggas doing wearing my ties?" He then frowned at Norcie and Martha and walked on into church. The boys stood perfectly still-shocked. The girls thought Carl was so mean. But, they'd taken his personal property to give as Christmas gifts.

The Bennett Clan sat in the same pew. Time rolled around for the invitation to discipleship. Carl prepared to stand, but Grandpa Dan quickly grabbed him by the arms.

"Sit down boy. Don't you go up there. If you ain't got the Holy Ghost by now, ya ain't gonna get it. Now, sit back. What ya doing anyway, that ya gotta keep going to the mourner's bench for, huh?"

Carl didn't reply and just slid back in his seat.

Later that night Grandpa was reading a paper, Grandma was sewing, and the kids were playing partners in dominoes. Norcie and Martha won. Carl became so enraged he knocked the table over, causing some of the dominoes to fly into the fireplace.

Grandpa Dan looked him dead in the eye and said, "Boy you better get every one of them out, and not one of them better be burnt."

Carl quickly rushed to the fireplace, plopped on his knees, and started grabbing dominoes. He was able to get all of them out with barely a scorched corner.

L.E. began to grin and laugh to himself then he remembered where he was. Finally, benediction came and services were dismissed. He waited outside for Essie to emerge from the building. As she came out, he approached her.

"Hi Essie. How are you?" he asked. They then began a casual conversation. She was to graduate that year and looking forward to moving on with her life. Though, she wasn't sure whether she'd go to college or move to a big city and find a job. Too many decisions to make. L.E. asked if she was seeing anyone. Last he heard she and one of his classmates, Elroy Perkins, had been an item. Essie stated no, she wasn't particularly interested in anybody at the present time. L.E. proceeded to ask her out to the movies on Saturday night.

She replied, "Yes!" She would stay in town at her grandfather's. L.E. could pick her up there. Their plans were made and they bid each other a good night, as the crowd dispersed.

On the way home, L.E. told his mother, "I think I've just met the girl that I'm going to marry."

"Oh, who?", Grandma Anice asked.

"Essie Lee Jones," replied L.E.

"Sure nuff, well I tell you one thing. She sure is a sweet girl, and she'll probably make you a real good wife. But, I didn't know you two were courting?"

L.E. went on to explain to his mother what had happened, and how he saw the bright aura around Essie as she stood in the choir stand. Grandma Anice chuckled, and told L.E. that Essie may very well be the one he'll marry.

I personally think this aura he commented on was his emotions of seeing this pretty light skinned girl, with ample hips and gorgeous shapely legs. Maybe, that's what Grandma Anice chuckled about.

L.E. was filled with anticipation for this date, and could hardly wait for Saturday night to roll around. Sure enough Saturday night rolled around, and L.E. put on some of his best clothes and cologne. You know, his right guard and his left guard, too. He walked to Mays Addition where Essie awaited his arrival. L.E. was invited in and spoke to her gathered family, then they were off to the Normana Theater. They enjoyed themselves at the movies. In those days, on the weekends, you would always have a double feature. Afterwards, he walked her the three miles back to her grandfather's house in Mays Addition. L.E. asked if he could see her again. She agreed, and promised to write once his leave was over. Of course, L.E. remembered his manners. The next day, he quickly went to see Essie's parents, Sallie and Dave Jones, and asked Mr. Jones for permission to court his daughter.

Mr. Jones not only gave his permission, but also gave L.E. some good advice. True, Mr. Jones knew Mrs. Anice Bennett and her family, which had a good reputation. However, Essie was his oldest daughter and well loved. Mr. Jones told L.E. that he was always to bring Essie home the same way he picked her up.

Granddad Dave said, "Essie is good and kind hearted, and he didn't want to have any trouble from L.E. If anything were to happen to Essie, he'd come looking for L.E. Essie's already been raised. If the two of them can't get along, then L.E. best bring her home, but don't he dare lay a hand on her."

L.E. acknowledged an understanding of this sound and good advice. He could see that this was a proud and loving family, such as his own. Essie's family history would prove to be just as interesting.

The Jones family history began with a priest from Spain, who immigrated to the United States. His name became David Thornton. He never told anyone exactly where he came from, as if it was some dark secret. There was speculation, however, because he was very well off for a minister of that time period. He settled near Cuero, Texas where he met and married Rosie Orange, a Creole. She did domestic work, and was the daughter of Mary Orange, a Blackfoot Indian, who bore Rosie in Louisiana. Rosie's father was of French descent. Together David and Rosie had four children. Piercie, Effie, Rosie, and Eric.

Effie was a strong stern looking lady with a healthy figure. Her complexion would darken during the summer months, and she'd look more like an Indian. She married a military man and bore two sons, one she named after her brother Eric.

Rosie was a light skinned, tall and lanky woman, like the cartoon character Olive Oil. She also married a military man, and they had no children.

Eric was dark skinned with pointed ears. As a child his hair was braided and his dress was almost like a girl's. He grew to be a handsome young man, well liked by the ladies. He entered the Army and after his discharge became a train porter. He never married and died from a ruptured appendix in his early thirties. His name sake nephew, Effie's son, would also die of the same fate.

While in town one day Piercie met a tall black farmer by the name of Andy Hamilton. It is not known why, but she was quite taken with him. Against her fathers wishes Piercie agreed to marry Andy. When Andy arrived at their home to pick her up, in his wagon, Granddad David was inflamed with anger. He cursed Andy and threatened to disown Piercie. David ran behind the wagon shouting his threats, if Piercie didn't return. Piercie waved to him, with tears streaming down her face, and shouted, "Father, I Love You." She then turned and continued on her journey with Andy.

A black farmer from El Campo, of little means, is not what David Thornton wanted for any of his girls. Especially, a widowed man, ten to twenty years her senior. But, Piercie was entranced with Andy and married without her father's blessings. David Thornton disowned her and never spoke to her again.

Piercie and Andy had five children, Andy Jr., David, Raymond, Rosie and Sallie. Piercie had a hard pregnancy with Sallie. The midwife did her best, but she lost a lot of blood. After the birth, Piercie became extremely ill. A combination of hypovolemia and likely an infection, and she died a few weeks later. Word reached David Thornton and he immediately took his dinky car to El Campo. By the time he arrived, it was too late. When he arrived Piercie was being buried. David felt Andy killed his young daughter by giving her the harsh life of a farmer's wife. He cursed Andy and left. Granddad David hated Andy for this and was very bitter, as well as, broken hearted. If he would have known of the illness in time, he could have held her hand and rubbed her head. Did she feel alone? Was she frightened? He eventually became very ill and died, still angry and bitter about Piercie.

Andy took in another woman to raise his children. Sallie grew healthy, but always had a longing to know her mother. Piercie's sisters, Rosie and Effie contacted the family, so the girls would know their mother's family. However, they weren't generous enough to take the girls in and raise them. Rosie and Effie were living a good life with plenty of money and nice things; whereas, little Rosie and Sallie had a hard farm life without their mother.

Sallie married Dave Jones, of Schulenburg, Texas. He was twenty years her senior, with two sons from a prior marriage, Ollie and Earlie. Sallie and Dave had six additional children-Essie, Joyce, Bernice, Leonard, Geneva, and Arthur. They were extremely poor, but well raised. Granddad Dave passed in 1964.

L.E. and Essie had a wonderful time together on their dates. He would say to himself, I'm not letting her go. He was going to hold on to this one. His leave was over the first part of April 1955. They were married September 20, 1955. Reverend A.A. Hargrove, Pastor of Mt. Olive Baptist Church, officiated over the ceremony at his own home. L.E. and Essie moved to San Antonio, Texas where they set up housekeeping. Essie first stayed with his sister, Norcie, while L.E. went to finish his tour. Then they both moved in with Carl and Eva, in the Wheatley Courts, on San Antonio's east side.

Essie was one of the brightest spots in L.E.'s life. A very loving, caring and sharing person. The qualities and values similar to his mother, in which he admired. She was sweet and giving, but would not allow herself to be used.

When Louis Ervin Bennett was born, January 27, 1956, L.E. was at Fort Lawton, Washington. His company basketball team had won their game. He was excited, but not as excited as he was when the phone call came. Norcie called from San Antonio and told him he was the father of a healthy baby boy, and both were doing fine. The next morning L.E. called to tell Essie he loved her and was anxious for his June 7, 1956 discharge date. L.E. named his first son because he didn't want him to endure the frustrations of only having initials.

L.E. was overwhelmed with his son and couldn't get enough of holding him. Louis cried every time because he was not familiar with his daddy. L.E. and Essie were blessed with four children, Louis Ervin, Sharon Kay, Kenneth Lyle, and Lisa Elizabeth. The boys are dark brown skinned like their daddy, and the girls are light brown like their mother, with big eyes, like their daddy. Their union has been a wonderful experience, even though they've gone through much together. He found her to be the person, when all else was going wrong, she would lend a calming voice to the situation and enable them to reach a clear and concise understanding. The marriage hasn't been perfect; there have been as many ups as downs, and many stresses that threatened the continuation of their marriage. During all his travels, union issues, and time in school there were no complaints, but a whole lot of understanding from Essie. The kids were always neat and clean, and well dressed. Essie could use coupons and second hand shops like it was nobody's business. She's an excellent cook, as well. She recognized that it was necessary for L.E. to acquire the education required for them to succeed in life. This kept him from spending time with the family, but it helped him obtain a better job. She has been his strongest supporter, and that's why L.E. considers her the Love of his life.

## I NEVER DREAM

I never knew with whom all my dreams
would come true,
Now I know, because God blessed me
with you.
Someone to share all the seasons in time
Someone who would only be mine,
Now I know that all the while
For whom I was waiting,
When I saw your smile.
You have changed my life with the warmth
of your love, and with you I feel safe.
This is the beginning of all we will share
to you I want to give myself.
Two separate people, joined by one beautiful love.

**SHARON BENNETT-WILLIAMS (2000)**

# CHAPTER V

It's job hunting time. L.E. was discharged from the Army June of 1956 and applications were placed everywhere, but no job offers came. L.E. and Essie did not have much money, so they spent time going to the drive-inn movies. They just wanted some time alone and to enjoy each other.

L.E. never lost focus on the fact that he needed a job. One day as the sun began to sink slowly in the west, and the breeze began to blow on a typical hot summer day; L.E. and Essie decided to visit Martha and Ruel, her husband. They took a nice slow stroll over on Onslow Street; with the baby in L.E.'s arms. They sat out in the backyard swapping tall tales. Martha asked how was the job hunting going. L.E. responded that he hadn't found anything worthwhile, yet. Martha asked if he'd put an application in at the telephone company. L.E. hadn't even thought about that. However, he certainly didn't mind giving it a try. Martha's neighbor worked for them and said it was a good place to work.

The very next day, L.E. went downtown to Southwestern Bell Telephone Company. He was greeted at the employment office by a Mrs. Margaret Mitchell. L.E. explained that he was interested in placing an application for a job. Mrs. Mitchell told him that she'd be glad to take his application, but couldn't promise him anything, right away. Once he completed the form, she reviewed it and thanked him for considering Southwestern Bell. Mrs. Mitchell told L.E. that all they had to offer a colored person, was janitorial work, or a garage-man position, which only paid three dollars a week more than a house-serviceman. She wanted to know if he'd be interested.

There was silence, as L.E. thought to himself, "Is this how they do it? Take the application, say they couldn't promise anything, then act like they're doing you a favor by offering a possible janitorial position?"

Mrs. Mitchell further exclaimed, she was sorry they didn't have something better to offer. But, who knows there may be something better later on. However, that's not a promise, you understand. "If you're interested Mr. Bennett, you'd need to take a physical exam, and if you pass we'll talk about hiring?"

A few days later L.E. received a call to go to the Medical Arts Building for his examination. Later he received another call to go back down to the employment office. Mrs. Mitchell told him there was an opening at the Pershing Central Office for a house-serviceman, and that there were other candidates being considered for the position. Would he still be interested?

L.E. replied in the affirmative. Thinking, that position was just fine to start. She then asked him if he had any relatives working with the company?

L.E. responded, "No."

Mrs. Mitchell just wondered because the companies best referrals usually came from current employees. She gave L.E. his folder and told him to take it over to Mr. Sid Cline at the Pershing Central Office. Mr. Cline would review the information and notify the main office of his decision. L.E. found Mr. Cline's office on the second floor of the building. He was interviewed and told that he would be notified in a few days. A few days passed and L.E. was requested to report for work at the Pershing Central Office with Mr. Cline as his 2nd line manager. The north district office was housed in this building.

L.E. was hired on June 21, 1956, and was now a Southwestern Bell Telephone employee. He considered himself fortunate to have been hired by such a reputable company. The Bell companies had proven to be an asset to the community, state, and the nation.

Whenever you told someone that you worked for the telephone company, they would most likely say, "You have a good job."

L.E. began as a house-serviceman (janitor). However, he had no intentions of staying in that position forever. He had plans, big plans, and that was to get his foot in the door and then make what he wanted. He was determined to move up.

Mr. John Murphy was the District Manager, Mr. Cline was his second level manager, and W.W. Schultz was his first line supervisor. They were all very cordial men and eager to get L.E. acclimated to the job.

Mr. Schultz was a tall blondish haired man, who's grin stretched from ear to ear. He would always greet you with a strong, warm handshake, and a big smile. After explaining to L.E. the nature of the job, Schultz then took him downstairs to meet his coworkers- Philip, Martin, and Louis Polk. These three men had a great sense of humor, and they knew their jobs very well. They proved to be a great asset to L.E. in the long run. Schultz designated Martin and Polk as being responsible for teaching L.E. the ropes. The men were then left alone to get on with the business of the day. Uniforms were ordered for L.E., so he would be in compliance with company policy.

L.E. soon discovered that Martin had a really great sense of humor. On break, Martin would sit and tell one story after another. He would keep L.E. and Louis laughing, sometimes, until they would almost cry. Martin told a story about once having been caught speeding on a back country road.

A cop pulled him over and said, "Look boy, I clocked you speeding. You were doing fifty-five in a thirty-five mile per hour zone."

Martin said he never saw a speed limit sign, and didn't believe that he was speeding.

The police officer said, "Well, I'm not going to argue with you about that. If you don't think you were speeding, then you can just go and tell it to the judge. So, just follow me and we'll go to see the judge."

Martin said, "Let's go. Because I know I wasn't speeding."

So, he got in his car and followed the officer to a stately looking mansion, sitting way back out in the country. It had a nice green rolling lawn. They pulled in front of the mansion, got out, and went inside. When they entered the house, the living room was set up like a court room, with the judge's bench, seating, and all. The police officer told Martin to have a seat, and the judge would be out in just a minute. Martin sat down to await the judge. Pretty soon the officer came out with a judge's robe on. He walked over behind the bench, and banged the gavel.

Saying, "Who comes before the court?"

Martin said, "I do your honor! How much do I owe you?" the whole group laughed.

It would not be long before L.E. would develop a pet name for Martin. He would start calling him, "The Ole Pro", after a cartoon character that was used in the old Falstaff Beer commercials, back in the fifties and sixties. Martin reminded L.E. so much of that character, that Martin even started calling himself, "The Ole Pro." The three of them developed a wonderful relationship and worked well together.

The employees relationship with their supervisor was good, also, and occasionally Schultz would take them out for employee anniversary celebrations. On one occasion, they went out to celebrate Melvin Porter's anniversary. They each had steak with jalapeno peppers. L.E., like his mother, loved spicy foods, so he had a ball with those peppers. Perhaps, one too many. He learned that moderation in all things was a good practice to follow; however, he managed to survive the night, and was no worse for wear on the next day.

It would not be long after his employment that L.E. would be approached by the Local Union President, Mr. U.S.G. Cyphers of Local #6131, the union that represented the minority members of Communication Workers of America (CWA), in San Antonio. L.E. spoke of his dreams for blacks to progress to positions other than as janitors. Mr. Cyphers invited him to become a member of the local union. L.E. joined and became an active member. He attended all meetings and got to know the other members. L.E. later met a member by the name of Ulysses S. Axiel, who would make an indelible impression upon him.

Axiel, who had a sterling personality, became one of L.E.'s most endearing friends. Sometimes, to just be helpful, Axiel picked L.E. up giving him a ride to and from work. Axiel was a chain smoker. He either had a cigar or a cigarette in his mouth. L.E. had stopped smoking by the time he was discharged, and hadn't given it a second thought since. But, in the mornings when Axiel picked him up, he'd always ask L.E. if he wanted a smoke. L.E. would reply, no. One day, on the way home, Axiel had a little snort under the front seat, and they both had a sip or two. This time when Axiel offered a smoke, L.E. replied, yes. L.E. started smoking on a regular basis, and began to buy cigarettes. At one point L.E. didn't have any more cigarettes of his own, and he asked Axiel to let him have a cigarette.

Axiel replied, "man, if you gonna smoke, you need to learn how to keep buying your own."

L.E. promptly reminded him that he was the one who kept offering him a smoke in the first place. They had a real big laugh about that.

## JOHN 15:12-13

This is my commandment,
That ye love one another, as I have loved you.
Greater love hath no man than this,
That a man lay down his life for his friends.

# CHAPTER VI

1957 was upon L.E. before he knew it, and another child was on the way. L.E. and Essie were hoping for a girl, because the first was a boy. They had planned on four children, two boys and two girls. On May 3, 1957, Sharon Kay was born at Hicks Lying Hospital on South Hackberry Street, in San Antonio, TX. L.E. named her Sharon Kay after Sharon Kay Ritchie, who was Miss. Texas in the Miss. America competition. Sharon was a beautiful, fat, gray-eyed, little girl with big dimples in her cheeks when she smiled. She had a smile that just warmed her daddy's heart. But in a time of exhaustion and under intense stress, he would hurt the face of the little girl with the smile that warmed her daddy's heart.

The Bennett's had been blessed with two beautiful and healthy children. Louis would grow to look so much like L.E. as a young man. Sharon possessed her father's temperament, but had her mother's tenderness.

One month after Sharon's birth, L.E. enrolled in the summer session at St. Phillips Junior College. He wanted to further his education and find a place to rent for his growing family. He and Essie had moved once already from his brother Carl's, to a duplex on Blaine Street, just off New Braunfels Street on the Eastside. Charles and Mercie Pitts lived on the other side of the duplex. They were a young couple with children, as well. These two young families shared the bathroom, and became friends and good neighbors.

Essie joined Mt. Calvary Baptist Church of San Antonio prior to L.E.'s discharge from the Army, so he joined as well. He knew Rev. B.F. Langham from his days as the revivalist for Mt. Olive Baptist Church in El Campo, one hundred miles from San Antonio. The young Bennett family lived in the duplex for just a short while, before they moved to a small rental house on Yucca Street, where they lived when Sharon was born.

Grandma Anice sold her home in El Campo and came to live with L.E. and Essie, until she was able to find her own home on Hays Street. Grandma Anice joined the Mt. Calvary church family, too.

Time was moving fast. The kids were growing like weeds and L.E. became more involved in union activities, and trying to keep pace with school. These were becoming difficult times for L.E., working eight hours a day and going to school three nights a week. He got up early each morning, around five a.m. to catch a bus to work, where he had to report in at six a.m. He would get off at three p.m., and catch the bus to St. Philips, get out of class around nine thirty p.m., and catch the bus home. Which was the last bus for the night, and if he missed it, he was in big trouble. He made certain he was on that last bus. He arrived home around eleven thirty p.m. This meant hurrying from class to catch it at Nebraska Street, now known as Martin Luther King Drive. It took him downtown in time to make the connection for the bus home. So, whenever Axiel gave him a ride to and from work, it was greatly appreciated, and helped make for a better day. The summer of 1958, L.E. enrolled again for night school at St. Philips, in pursuit of his business degree. He attended under the G.I. Bill.

One day at work, a white employee asked L.E. if he were attending school on the company tuition plan. L.E. said that he wasn't, and didn't know about such a plan. The white employee told him to check with his supervisor, so he could get financial assistance. L.E. followed through, and sure enough he received forms to complete. Before long the assistance began. It would prove to be a great help to their household budget. Now they were able to stretch their dollars a little bit further.

Things were going well on the job. He knew his job well, and received regular merit increases. Now, L.E. and Essie were looking to buy a house. Essie saw an ad in the newspaper and it sounded perfect, and was on the bus route. This was important since they still had no car. Essie was pregnant with their third child. Who was born prior to their moving into this new home.

L.E. called his brother Floyd, who gave them a ride over to meet the owner. Mrs. Bellinger met them at 1314 Ervin Street and showed them around. Everyone loved the house. It was a small white home, with living room, kitchen, two bedrooms, one bathroom, and no garage. They told Mrs. Bellinger they desired to purchase the property. The owner explained that no changes could be made to the property without her prior approval, and that once it was paid for in full, the deed would then be transferred to them. L.E. and Essie could hardly contain themselves, they were so excited about the prospect of home ownership.

L.E. borrowed the funds from the company credit union, and they then moved in. Essie was as happy as any woman could be in her own home. Some of the most pleasant family memories about Ervin Street were when Grandma Anice came and spent time, especially, after church, on Sundays. She enjoyed sitting in the backyard and watching Louis and Sharon play. L.E. would tell her of his hopes and dreams. He wanted to advance on his job, but minorities weren't allowed to bid for the entry-level craft jobs. If you were Black, then you were stuck in the positions of garage-man or house-servicemen and house-servicewomen. He constantly brought the subject up in union meetings, but nothing was done to try and change things.

L.E. was a young man; a man of hope, of vision, of promise, and of integrity. To him the current union leaders weren't willing to take up, or press the issue of minorities not being able to bid on craft jobs. They were simply doing what they knew, going along with the status quo, and not rocking the boat. L.E. was considering running for president of the Communications Workers of America, local union #6131. Grandma Anice voiced her concern of him having too much on his plate already. But if a change was to be made, someone had to take a stand and do what was necessary. Maybe that person was him.

It was August 13, 1959, around eleven o'clock at night and Essie began to have birth pains. L.E. took her to Robert B. Green Hospital, and at approximately one a.m., August 14, 1959, a beautiful bouncing baby boy was born. The nurse, Earline, who was Floyd's wife at the time, went to the waiting room and asked L.E. if he wanted to see his baby boy. She then said that they may have gotten the babies mixed up somehow, because he looked too much like a Mexican baby. Maybe L.E. should get him checked out. But he was not a little Mexican, he was an African-American baby, and just as cute as a button. His name was Kenneth Lyle Bennett.

The Bennett's now had three children. Two boys and a girl. Things were moving along with a precise smoothness, as far as family planning was concerned. Grandma Anice was all smiles when she saw the baby. She nicknamed him, "Dumas," because of the T.V. commercial from Dumas Milner Chevrolet, and its animated character. She loved that commercial. Soon sibling rivalry set in, and Louis and Sharon complained that Kenneth was getting too much attention. Even though they could not verbalize it their actions clearly signaled that they felt neglected from the usual treatment that they'd become accustomed to receiving. But by now Essie Lee was well aware of what was going on, and she knew how to handle the problem, because she had dealt with it before, when Sharon arrived.

L.E. graduated with honors, the summer of 1960, from St. Philips Jr. College, with an associates in Business Administration. Tommie Lee Steadham was the class valedictorian. Essie sat in the auditorium, while L.E. received his certificate. She was as proud of his achievements as he was. Anice, who had struggled to see him through high school, and now with her health failing she wasn't able to physically attend, but she was there spiritually. L.E. remembers those days at St. Philips, sometimes grueling hours of study to ensure a final good grade. L.E. was determined to get all he had earned.

Graduation day was a great experience for him. The graduation sermon was preached by Dr. S.H. James, pastor of the Second Baptist Church. His theme was "Test All Things, and Prove what is Good", Romans 12:2." It was an outstanding message. The graduating class left Second Baptist Church with their heads held high. Look out world, here they come. There was no stopping them now, another milestone had been reached! This was quite an accomplishment. He was the first and only member of his family to graduate high school, and now junior college. This would mean more income and a better future for him and his family, but his greatest sacrifices were yet to come.

L.E. continued in school, having enrolled at St. Mary's University, in September of 1960. He was going to earn a Bachelors in Business Administration and Marketing. His first meeting at St. Mary's was with Brother George B. Kohennon, Dean of the School of Business. He was a middle aged man with graying hair and horn rimmed glasses. After cordial introductions and handshakes, the Dean asked L.E. to take a seat. Dean Kohennon then asked L.E. why he wanted to be a Marketing major in the field of Business.

L.E. replied, "that it has been a desire of his to be successful in the field of business. L.E. wanted to be a top flight manager with some successful company, and hopefully, someday own a successful business of his own."

Dean Kohennon's rejoinder was, "Well, I think that is admirable on your part, to have such high expectations, but I think you need to be realistic. I doubt seriously that any firm would be willing to hire you as a manager. There doesn't seem to be a desire to hire Negro managers. You will probably have to seek employment in some of the northern states, or else stick with the Black professions. Such as medicine, law, or school teaching for Blacks."

L.E. reiterated that his desire was to be a manager. Not a lawyer, doctor, nor school teacher. Personally, he didn't see why he should have to go up north to find a job, when he was born and raised right there in Texas. He also didn't see why he should have to leave his home state when there must be jobs available right there. The Dean went on to tell L.E. that St. Mary's University does have a very fine School of Business, and L.E. would have a nice stay there. But it was his duty to explain the facts to him as he saw them. L.E. thanked him for his candor.

L.E.'s life had become disorganized and tumultuous, with his responsibilities with the union, and studies at school. He purchased his textbooks, and started classes. L.E. was full of excitement about being at St. Mary's University. He found the instructors cordial, helpful, but demanding; just as they should have been. Never once did he experience any difference in attitude from classmates or the instructors. It was a catholic college, and the majority of instructors were catholic priests, nuns, and brothers or sisters. He recalled quite vividly, a particular incident one beautiful fall evening, when he reported to his first marketing class. The instructor was Mr. William Peery, who was a slender, moderately built gentleman with a heavy shock of grey hair, and spoke with a slight lisp. The instructor apparently loved horseback riding, because he very often would come to class dressed in his riding habit. A grey Stetson, set somewhat to the left side of his head, with his riding jacket, riding pants, spit shined boots, and crop. They could hear him coming down the hallway, and they knew it would not be long before he entered the door.

On that opening night of class, Mr. Peery felt it was necessary to have the students understand something-he was going to be a taskmaster. He further stated, that in his class room, there would be no A's. As far as Mr. Peery was concerned, the author of the class book is the "A", Mr. Peery is the "B", and the most the students can expect is a "C". The class knew they were in for a rough ride. He was tough, but fair. Mr. Peery didn't mind explaining how the cow ate the cabbage, and would give students helpful hints, to move them in the right direction. The class was enjoyable, but the instructor wanted results.

L.E.'s class work wasn't faring as well as it could have been, because his attention was so badly divided. He would take office as President of Local Union #6131, in January 1961. Lawrence H. Randle was Vice President, John F. Rucker was treasurer, and Ulyssess A. Axiel was chief steward. He was also changing central offices on his job. The telephone company operated that way. It moved employees around, so that when someone went on vacation, an employee wouldn't be a complete stranger to that office. Being low in seniority, it was expected of L.E. to take those new assignments. The worse part was having to work some Sundays, which kept him from attending church with his family. He really missed that. The worst assignment entailed working out at Lackland Air Force Base, because of the distance, not because of the other employees.

Mr. Moses Williams, Mrs. Stiewig, and the other ladies at the air base were always cordial, and as helpful as they could be. But with no transportation of his own, it made things really difficult.

Mr. Williams would give him a ride out to the city bus stop, so L.E. could catch the bus back to the east side of town; sometimes he would even give him a ride home. It saved a lot of walking for him. However, each day impressed upon L.E. that he really needed a car. During his break time, he started looking through the newspaper. He found a car lot for used vehicles on West Commerce Street, and the bus went right by it on the way home. After work one day L.E. was determined to purchase a car. If the terms were right for what he could afford, then he'd buy a car. On his way home he got off the bus across the street from the lot. It had been raining heavily on and off all week and this time it was pouring rain. The car dealer had a little hut in the middle of a lot, close to Our Lady of the Lake College, near West Commerce and S.W. 24th Street. L.E. walked over to the hut, and of course, they were glad to see him. The two young Hispanic salesmen were eager to sell him a car. They showed L.E. around and he finally decided on a 1951 Chevy, black, four door. L.E. asked if he could take it for a drive. The young men he was dealing with were most agreeable. L.E. attempted to start the engine, but the engine would not turn over.

The salesman said, "Oh, it just needs a little jump, and it will start right up."

He retrieved his battery charger, and hooked it up. In a few minutes, he told L.E. to give her a try. This time the engine started. L.E. took it for a drive, and it ran good, so he returned to the lot and negotiated a price. L.E. took the necessary papers for he and Essie to sign, stepped out of the little tin hut, got into the car, and again it wouldn't start.

"No problem, I'll just jump it, and you will be on your way", the salesman said. He jump started the car again, and L.E. was off and running.

L.E. drove through downtown and stopped at a red light, W. Houston and Santa Rosa Streets. When he stopped the engine died. He hit the starter, but the engine would not turn over. L.E. sat there for a while, trying to get the engine to start, but it would not start. He was frustrated, tired, exhausted from school, and he really wanted and needed a car. He finally took the keys and placed them under the front floor mat. He got out of the car, locked the doors, and went to a pay phone across the street to call the dealer.

The salesperson said, "No problem, I will be right there and give you a jump, and that will get you going again."

L.E. told him that wouldn't be necessary. "Your car papers are in the glove compartment, your keys are under the front floor mat on the drivers side, and the doors are locked. I'm catching the bus home." L.E. hung up the phone. That Saturday, He went downtown to Bexar Motors and purchased a 1951 gray Dodge four door. He drove it until times got better. You couldn't stop L.E. Bennett now, he was moving up in the world.

## BE PATIENT

All is not what it seems,
the world may seem so mean.
Give things time, have patience and wait.
When the time is right, things will be straight.
Don't rush God, Don't rush fate,
Just be patient, and wait!

Sharon Bennett-Williams (01/01)

# WELCOME

# TO THE

# BENNETT/JONES FAMILY

# ALBUM/SCRAPE BOOK

ANNICE I. BENNETT, HER LATE 30's

WEBB BENNETT                    MACK BENNETT

CARL BENNETT

LLOYD BENNETT

FLOYD BENNETT & WIFE JANIE

RAY BENNETT

HATTIE MAE & HUSBAND WILLIAM

NORCIE BENNETT

MARTHA(above) DAN"s sisters(right)

L.E. AT 15

(right) L.E. IN ARMY

RAY BENNETT IN NAVY, LOOKING
SUAVE, AND AT HIS WEDDING TO
Doris.

annice, later years

FANNIE FRANCIS VINSON
ANNICE'S GERMAN GRANDMOTHER

sister-Catherine(cat)

sister-Gladys

EPFIE,MARTHA(midwife),& Jessie          PEARL, ANNICE'S AUNT(FATHER'S SID
not shown.  Maggie Brown-Parson
& Babe. (ANNICE'S AUNTS)

L.E.   &RAY ON LEAVE

L.E. IN KOREA

L.E. CENTER & PACE
FRONT.

DAVID THORNTON
Rosie Orange Thornton(below)

DAVID THORNTON PRIOR TO DEATH
Piercie Thornton (below)

Eric Thornton as a child

ERIC AS A TEENAGER

EFFIE THORNTON AS A TEEN
(below)

EFFIE IN HER LATE  50's
(below)

Rosie as a child 1901

Rosie & a suitor (below)

Rosie & her Husband

Rosie & Effie(below)

ANDY HAMILTON

PIERCE'S DAUGHTERS' ROSIE HAMILTON(LEFT) AND
SALLIE (right)
JONE'S FAMILY BELOW, DAVE JONES AT HEAD OF TABLEPRAYING

ESSIE  LEE  JONES

L.E. BENNETT

### Greer Seniors To Graduate Thur.

Four Seniors of Greer High School will receive diplomas Thursday evening at 8 at the Greer School here. They are Valedictorian L. E. Bennett, Salutatorian Essie Jean Walker, and Robert Louis Bellis and Elroy Perkins.

O. A. Ray, principle of the J. H. Fox High School Jasper, will

be the commencement speaker. Roe is past president of the Texas Colored State Teachers Association.

The baccalaureate sermon was given last Sunday by Rev. R. J. Johns Baptist pastor from Elgin.

The Greer class had its entire banquet April 30

LEE ERNEST BENNETT          ELROY PERKINS

Photos by Connie's Studio

L.E. & ESSIE AFTER MARRIAGE

## Labor Leader Cries "Phony!"

**PHONEY PHRASE SAYS LOCAL LEADER**

In view of the recent statements of Joe Scott regarding discrimination in Unions and the Greater Bexar County State of legislators' endorsement of the "Right-To-Work" laws, SNAP interviewed L. E. Bennett prominent local labor leader on these matters.

Mr. Bennett, President of Local 6131 Communications Workers of America, told SNAP, "This matter of the so called 'Right - to-Work' law is another example of phoney phrases. The law gives no man any right to work. Nor does it creat any work. It is merely another example of management and the power structure using a misleading title to delude the uninformed public. Actually any fair management prefers to deal with an enlightened union rather than endure the chaos of an unorganized labor force. It is only those who seek to keep starvation wages and sub-standard working conditions in effect who advocate this UNION-BUSTING type of legislation. Believe me, I know—ORGANIZED LABOR IS THE ONLY HOPE FOR THE WORKING MAN."

greetings from President L. B. Johnson who communicated his apologies for not being able to attend the recent birthday party for Rudy Esquivel.

Scenes from the birthday party held for State Representative Rudy Esquivel, in the Villa Fontana, 403 South Alamo, Wednesday March 18, 1964. The picture (l. to r.) L. E. Bennett,labor man; Gill Douss, Assistant D. A.; Judge Peter Curry and Assistant D. A. Carl Hill and his wife.

ESSIE WITH LOUIS & SHARON

LOUIS, SHARON, & KENNETH
(BENNETT CHILDREN)

ESSIE WITH SHARON

ESSIE WITH THE KIDS
(SHARON KENNETH, & LOUIS

SHARON & louis

LOUIS ERVIN BENNETT( FIRST BORN)

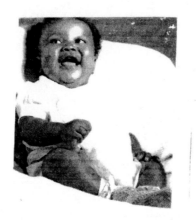

SHARON KAY BENNETT (SECOND BORN)

SHARON WITH THE ANGEL RING.

KINDERGARTEN GRADUATION

KENNETH LYLE BENNETT

HIGH SCHOOL GRADUATION

KENNETH'S LAST PHOTOGRAPH

A ELIZABETH BENNETT, THROUGH THE YEARS

ERIC SITTING HOOD OF DINKY CAR, WITH FRIENDS.
(below) ROSIE & SUITOR

EFFIE DURING SUMMER MONTHS

LOUIS WITH SHARON, WHO'S TRYING
TO DRINK AND STAND(WHAT A CHORE)

ANNICE WITH LOUIS & SHARON          EASTER SHARP!

(LEFT) LOUIS, SHARON, KENNETH
(BELOW) KENNETH & LOUIS

ESSIE & L.E.
WITH KIDS,
PLAYLAND PAR
IN
SAN ANTONIO

(L TO R.) ESSIE,MITT,FLOYD, & L.E.
ENJOYING A NIGHT FROM UNION DUTIES.

L.E. PRESENTED WITH LIONS AWARD

Judge Alan Warrick was the guest speaker at the last
week Alamo City Lions Club meeting held at Health,
Inc. The Judge is shown with, left, club president
L.E. Bennet.

# Dr. James Northcutt is Lions Speaker

Seated left to right, Essie Bennett, past president Alamo Lioness Club; Des Moines Jones, past president Alamo City Lioness Club. Standing left to right, L.E. Bennett, past president Alamo City Lions Club; Howard Fox, zone chairman VIB, Ernesto "T.J." Tijerina, district governor 2-A2; James Northcutt, M.D., member Alamo City Lions Club (rear); Manuel "Manny" Zamora, lt. governor district 2-A2 and Aquila McGrew, immediate past president of Alamo City Lions Club.

Alamo City, Lioness Club attended the Lincoln West Banquet from left are Lionesses Birdie Coleman, Sarah McGrew, Marvinette Smith, Essie Bennett, William Wallace, president of Lincoln West Lions, L.E. Bennett, president of Alamo City Lions, Bernice Evans, Louise

L.E. & ESSIE AFTER HIS
GRADUATION, B.A. IN THEOLOGY.

*Rev. L. E. Bennett, pastor of Galilee Baptist Church receives*
*Honorary Doctor of Divinity Degree*

L.E. BENNETT AS PASTOR                    ESSIE LEE BENNETT

FAMILY REUNION TIME. (L-R)
L.E., ESSIE, WEBB, & MARTHA

L.E. AND ESSIE AT A LIONS/LIONESS BANQUET

ESSIE'S SIBLINGS. (standing) Leonard & Arthur(l-r)

(L-R) Bernice,Joyce,Geneva, & Essie

## How a club
## aids East Side

In a continuing effort to keep the East Side community informed of its community involvements, the Alamo City Lions Club announced its contributions for the year of 1984.

The Alamo City Lions Club is a service organization and member of Lions International. We are actively involved in our community and the provisioning of various services in the way of help for crippled children, diabetes, the blind and eyeglasses for the needy.

The following contributions reflect our community concern: Health, Inc., $440; Boys Club, $100; YMCA, $100; eyeglasses (needy), $165.20; Henry Logan Heart Fund, $100; BCOIC, $30; Herb Petry Foundation Sports Complex, $500; and Texas Lions Camp, $280.

Every effort is being made to increase our contributions to the community in a manner that will be beneficial to all segments.

**—L.E. BENNETT**
Vice president
Alamo City Lions Club

L.E. & ESSIE ON NEW ORLEANS TRIP. ONE OF MANY, ENJOYING THE FRUITS OF THEIR YEARS OF LABOR.

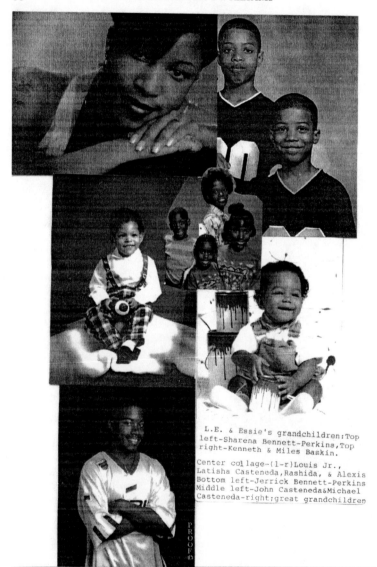

L.E. & Essie's grandchildren:Top left-Sharena Bennett-Perkins,Top right-Kenneth & Miles Baskin.

Center collage-(l-r)Louis Jr., Latisha Casteneda,Rashida, & Alexis Bottom left-Jerrick Bennett-Perkins Middle left-John Casteneda&Michael Casteneda-right;great grandchildren

# CHAPTER VII

L.E. loved being a union member, because he felt part of something important. A part of an organization that can effect a change for its people. He participated at every meeting with questions and suggestions. Most of his concerns centered around ways to advance positions for blacks within the company. L.E. was well dressed, well read, popular, and had a great presence. There was a fire building within him that the others could see. It would be these qualities that would lead union members to nominate him for President of local #6131.

L.E.'s nomination came during the same time John F. Kennedy was running for President of the United States. Civil Rights had come off the back burner and was receiving a prominent place in the minds of Americans. Dr. Martin L. King, Jr., Stokley Carmichael, Whitney Young, James Farmer, Thurgood Marshall, Roy Wilkins and others who were heating things up on the Civil Rights front, and they were seen in newspaper headlines across the country.

John F. Kennedy was saying all the right things. L.E. never forgot seeing him up close with Lyndon B. Johnson, during the 1960 presidential campaign while addressing a large crowd of people, in front of the Alamo. L.E. was enthralled as he stood and listened to his speech. The sincerity in his voice, as he spoke about opportunities for everyone gave L.E. great hope. Mr. Kennedy's face was red, from exposure to the sun, his blondish hair glistened in the sunlight. He was something to see, his speech was extremely impressive. To L.E.,

Mr. Kennedy had a magnetism about him that caused you to like him and want to follow him. He gave off a sincere feeling about what he expected to achieve, and L.E. wanted to become part of the process. A process that would help make this great nation of ours a nation where all people could share in the blessings of this wonderful country, regardless of ethnicity, the color of your skin, or where a person came from. L.E. felt he had a right to be included: if a person was already part of the process, they knew they had made the right choice. L.E. was motivated by John F. Kennedy's speech, and L.E. left that meeting in downtown San Antonio headed for home with a new determination to do something for the Black employees at the telephone company. He would not be just a token union president. He would be responsible for making things better for the union members and their families. He would work to open up opportunities for all. This was the first time he'd seen a man who was running for the office of President of the United States. L.E. became a life long Democratic Party supporter. L.E.'s life had now taken on new meaning. Not only did things need to change, they must change. He no longer had to immerse himself in wishful thinking, but he could do something to help make it happen. L.E. and J.F. Kennedy were campaigning for president of their own perspective offices, in different locations. John F. Kennedy had no personal knowledge of this man whose life he had affected, but L.E. was changed none the less. It was time for the torch to be passed from the old guard at the union, to a younger generation and progress must be made. Promises would be a thing of the past, and only concrete results would be accepted.

J. F. Kennedy made good on his promise, too. Shortly after being inaugurated as President of the United States, he issued an Executive Order requiring all companies doing business with the Federal Government to begin programs toward eliminating discrimination in the work place. Hearing this gave L.E. the opportunity necessary to approach the company about abiding by this order, once he became president.

There was a war now raging in America. That was the war

against segregation and racism. Not only for African-Americans but all people were being challenged to take a stand and not allow the continued hatred, degradation, and injustice of segregation and racism to continue. L.E. was now impassioned, and there was no turning back. There was an awakened realization within him that as an African-American he was entitled to all the bounty this country had to offer. He could no longer go along just to get along. He had rights that extended beyond simply working only the jobs white Americans allowed him to. L.E. was born and raised in this country called America. America was the land of opportunity for everyone who refused to be limited by the old, artificial boundaries of the color of a man's skin. L.E. was determined to break every boundary imposed by white Americans, and reach for every available opportunity. L.E.'s plan was to complete his education, so he could better meet various job qualifications. L.E.'s battle was to forge integration in entry-level craft jobs at Southwestern Bell. To have Blacks Americans, Latin Americans, and others placed in these entry-level positions, instead of only being garage-men, or house-servicemen and women.

L.E. was every bit as smart, as talented, as hard working and blessed with ambition. He was going to do more with his life than sweep floors. He would take advantage of education and earn the right to advance.

L.E. never saw Dr. Martin L. King, Jr. in person, only on television. For L.E. to sit and watch Martin L. King, Jr. made him feel good to be black. M.L.K. represented all that was good about what blacks wanted to achieve. When Martin spoke with a forcefulness, and mannerisms that reached out and grabbed L.E. by the throat, and pulled him, mentally into the fray of working to obtain opportunity for all. M.L.K. like J.F.K., was a handsome fellow with polished speeches that captivated audiences.

L.E. was impressed by J. F. K.'s preciseness and timeliness. L.E., would rather be an hour ahead of time, than to be a minute late. Time, to him, was of the essence. One only had so much of it to use, and how you used it could very well determine your success or failure. Be precise. Say what you mean, and mean what you say. To L.E. this was the epitome of John Kennedy.

But, M. L. K. was more deliberative. When one listened to him speak, it was as though he was deliberating some matter of crucial importance. Martin's concern seemed wrapped up in the struggle of men and women, who had been denied freedom of opportunity for centuries. It was as if Martin could hear the cry of unborn generations crying they will not be denied any longer. The expression in his voice bore the pain of W.E.B Dubois, Booker T. Washington, Sojourner Truth, Harriet Tubman, and Frederick Douglass, who longed for the things that Dr. King vocalized. He cried out to L.E. that he was standing at the door of opportunity, and that he had been denied too long. L.E. knew what was required of him. Duty had called. L.E. had been beckoned by two men he began to admire.

John F. Kennedy had given him the candle, and Martin L. King had furnished the fuel for ignition. L.E.'s continued obligation was apparent. There were people who needed better jobs and God had gifted L.E. with the talent to get the task done. This would be his mission.

Like Christ, every man should have a cause in life for which he'd be willing to die for. Our souls were worth dying for, and Christ came willingly to pay the price of our sins for all mankind. Each of us must, within ourselves, determine what path we will follow, and by the Grace of God, follow that path we must, until the job is done. Paul says, in Galatians 6:9, "And let us not be weary in well doing: for in due season we shall reap, if we faint not." L.E. firmly believed in the old adage that said, "anything worth doing, is worth doing right." Those two men lit a fire in L.E.'s soul, and even today, the fire still burns bright, because we still have a ways to go. L.E. had also reached a point in his life where he felt the Lord was going to let him alone about that preaching business that had been revealed to him as a child. So, he plunged ahead.

After being sworn in, January 1961, as the CWA's President of local union #6131, L.E. began a letter writing campaign to the division heads of the phone company, in San Antonio. He requested an audience to discuss the possibilities of obtaining some promotions for minorities from the house-service positions.

San Antonio was the South Texas area, which covered Laredo to Houston, and Austin to Corpus Christi. The headquarters were in Houston, TX.

The division level was as high as one could go in San Antonio. The division heads were Mr. C.C. Pervier, Division Plant Manager; Mr. Haywood, Division Traffic Manager; Mr. L.H. Hudson, Division Commercial Manager; and Mr. Hughes, Div. Accounting Manager. L.E. sat down to his black Underwood typewriter at the kitchen table, which Essie had given to him for Christmas. He'd learned to type while at St. Philips, and this typewriter would become a tremendous asset to him. He typed letters to all the division heads, as well as President Kennedy, and Robert Kennedy. While all responses were prompt and cordial, they were by telephone or word of mouth. Eventually, March 1961, L.E. was granted an audience. L.E. was accompanied by Randle, vice-president, Rucker, treasurer, and Axiel, the chief steward on each visit. As president, L.E. did do the talking.

The union officers met, prior to all company meetings, and it was L.E.'s fervent desire that their decorum be impeccable, intelligent, and to the point. They did not receive a rebuff at these early meetings, but were informed that the journey would not be an easy one.

Mr. Haywood had expressed some reservations about hiring black telephone operators, because of the close proximity they would be with the white operators. He was concerned about their ability to get along on the job. But he never said that it wouldn't happen. The union members left each meeting some what uplifted, because their proposals were not flatly rejected. L.E. knew the struggle would be hard, but that the goal was achievable.

He continued his quest with letters asking that house-servicemen and women be considered for openings, along with all of the other employees. There was a daily watch of job announcements, in order to be knowledgeable about where openings existed. L.E.'s determination and dedication was so great that he took his typewriter down to the union hall on Saturdays. He would type letters for every house-service person who desired to have a better paying job in the craft ranks. Every letter needed to be legible and presentable. He would continue this until all union member requests had been filled. There were a good number of young employees who came forth to get their letters written. Finally, after all other request had been completed, L.E. wrote a letter for himself, asking consideration for a job in the Commercial Department, as a Business Representative (clerk type job). Since the Commercial and Plant were two different departments, there would have to be a hearing on the matter at the area headquarters level. L.E. had typed one hundred letters for civil rights meetings and job requests. Mind you L.E. was still attending evening classes, part time, at St. Mary's. The hearing was scheduled and Ulysses Axiel, and Mr. Paul Gray, a representative of the District Director for the C.W.A. National Union, attended with L.E. The two met with Mr. Kirkpatrick, the General Commercial Manager. Representing the general plant manager was Mr. Paul Parker, the area Plant Personnel Supervisor. The meeting began in a very cordial manner, and continued to move civilly, for a while. Mr. Kirkpatrick stated his position clearly as he saw it from the Commercial Departments stand point. Of course, he said, they were looking for good people.

Then Mr. Paul Parker said to L.E., "As far as I'm concerned, if I were your supervisor, I would fire you for not doing a good job where you are right now."

At that point L.E. stood up and banged his fist on the desk. L.E. stated, "How in the hell can I do any better a job then I'm already doing? The building that I'm responsible for maintaining, has just received the highest rating that General Headquarters gives on building inspection, and you can't do any better than that?"

L.E. was then led away by Axiel and Paul into the hallway to calm down. The meeting reconvened and Mr. Parker suggested L.E. go back and discuss it with his supervisor, because there was a bad appraisal in his file. However, L.E. felt that there was no such negative appraisal submitted by his supervisor, it was just another smoke screen they were using to delay efforts to integrate. It was company policy to review appraisals with each employee, and then have the employee sign. This is how his supervisor had done it in previous years. So, L.E. proceeded as though it had never happened, because he had no knowledge of any such appraisal.

Liken unto a huge dark forest full of plush green trees, whose limbs stretch forth to cover the soil under them, comes forth many small lights, almost like gold fairy dust. But, they're not fairies! They are the blessed souls sent forth by our Lord and Savior to stand in the front and guide people in the right direction. Do you look up and wish you could catch one? Just like trying to catch a lighting bug when you were a kid. The souls were given their battle assignments and locations. Malcolm X started for the people of Islam, and eventually all people. With his territory focus in New York and Chicago. Martin Luther King, Jr. focused on Georgia, Alabama, and Mississippi, but would go wherever he was needed.

John F. Kennedy and Robert Kennedy were for all people of our Nation. Rev. Josea Williams was the Georgia area, and a supporter of Mr. King. Reverend L.E. Bennett was in Texas with the telephone company. Today's leading lighted souls are Reverend Jesse Jackson for the world. T.D. Jakes who primarily has the Dallas area, but now takes the Lords message all over. Rev. Jasper Williams, Jr. and Jasper Williams, III, and Joseph Williams are in the Atlanta area. The list goes on and on. We all have a baton to hold, with duties to perform both large and small. We are to hold that baton tight and run the race as far as we can, for as long as we can.

> Let not your heart be troubled: ye believe in God,
> Believe also in me. John 14:1
> We are troubled on every side, yet not distressed;
> We are perplexed, but not in despair,
> Persecuted, but not forsaken;
> Cast down, but not destroyed. II Corinthians 4:8-9
> Though I walk in the midst of trouble
> Though wilt revive me: Thou shalt stretch

Forth thine hand against the wrath
Of mine enemies, and thy right hand shall save me
Paslms 138:7
Come now, and let us reason together,
Saith the Lord. Isiah 1:18

# CHAPTER VIII

L.E. felt it was time to agitate, but he wasn't sure just how to go about it. He did know that more pressure needed to be applied. There were other options, such as picketing or asking others to disconnect their phone services. Until now the letters were simple bids for craft jobs, without any additional information.

On a warm Sunday afternoon, he and Grandma Anice were watching the kids play in the backyard, while Essie and baby Kenneth took a nap. He told his mother of his sleepless nights with his head full of what had taken place and his plans. L.E. told Grandma Anice about his anger of being undervalued and not respected by some white people, and how he'd have to control himself from making a violent move. How could he shake things up without risking what they've possibly gained? Grandma Anice's advice was to state the facts, and stick with the facts. Nothing more and nothing less. In other words the letter content should include some history about this employee who wishes to rise in the ranks. L.E. understood and knew exactly what to do. He would point out that these were loyal, dedicated, and diligent people. These same people had been given regular merit raises. So, if they were good enough to hire, to keep as an employee, and they were good enough for wage increases based on the merits of their service, then they were good enough to be promoted. If these employees weren't giving good service then why haven't they been fired? L.E.'s statements could always be verified via the personnel files, because this was hard evidence. This strategy became the backbone of his letter campaign. The company was told to promote good candidates, but if they weren't giving good service then why weren't they working to improve the poor employees. Now which way would the company go? Grandma Anice sat there shaking her head in agreement. L.E. gazed at his mother and realized something was different about her. She seemed somewhat listless and not as energetic. Her visits with the family had decreased from what they were accustomed to.

L.E. asked her, "Momma, is there anything wrong?"

She said, "Don't know baby. I just seem to be suffering with a whole lots of indigestion lately."

L.E. told her that they needed to get her to a doctor for a check up, so they can find out what was going on. Grandma Anice responded that just may well be what she'll have to do. This was the summer of 1960. Sometime later when Grandma Anice was visiting the family, she complained again about the indigestion. It was now the fall of 1960. L.E. suggested she try exercising more to help stimulate her digestive system. Maybe, she should go for short walks.

Grandma Anice said, "Yes, I think I'll walk down to the corner and back to see if that helps."

She got up and went down to the corner, which was a very short distance, and when she returned she was extremely exhausted. L.E. told her that they were going to see to it that she see a doctor right away, because something was wrong somewhere. He then called Norcie and Martha and asked them if they would go with Grandma Anice to Robert B. Green Hospital in the morning? They quickly agreed, and picked her up early the next morning. L.E. went to work at the Pershing Central Office at 6:00 a.m., as usual. The whole day passed, and L.E. had not heard a word from his sisters on their mother's condition. After work he went straight to the hospital to check on his mother. When he arrived, and found them sitting in a waiting room, they told him that she hadn't seen a doctor yet. L.E. was enraged as he went to the counter and asked for the charge nurse. The charge nurse came out and identified herself.

L.E. pointed to Anice, who was now slumped over in the chair, and said, "That's my mother, and she has been here since five thirty a.m. this morning, and no one has attended to her yet. I want somebody to see about my mother right away?"

The nurse was very apologetic, and said, "We will take care of her right away, Mr. Bennett. I don't know what could have gone wrong, but she will be seen now."

The nurse kept her word and called his mother in to be checked. She was then admitted to the hospital because her situation was indeed bad. The indigestion problems were really pancreatic cancer.

Rev. B.F. Langham came by to visit during her hospital stay and had prayer with her. Grandma Anice told him, "Rev. Langham, I'm not worried. My life is in the hands of God, and my ticket on that ship, has already been paid for, and I'm alright. You know, not only will I get to see my maker, but I'll get to see my loving Dan. You know that was my nigga."

Rev. Langham simply smiled. Grandma's illness lingered on for a while, but she had suffered in silence much too long. It was a Sunday Morning, on July 30, 1961, L.E. had awaken early, and went to visit his mother. He arrived at the hospital, parked his car, and hurriedly went inside. He stepped off the elevator, and started down the hallway to his mother's room, when Hattie Mae, his oldest sister, came up the hallway toward him with tears in her eyes.

L.E. asked her, "What's wrong Totah?"

She looked up at him and said, "Momma just left us."

The emotions that L.E. felt were indescribable. He wanted to holler and scream, but his maleness would not allow him to do so. This heart wrenching pain was unbearable. He felt as if someone had pierced his chest with their fist, and yanked his heart out. He just held his sister for a while, then he released her, and walked into the room where his mother lay. L.E. kissed her on the forehead as he held her hands still warm in death. He looked at her hands. She had such lovely little fat hands, with curved pinkies. He always admired his momma's little fat hands, and he bent over to kiss the hands that once cradled him as a baby. He could not hold back the tears, any longer. Momma was gone! This beautiful, proud, gentle, sweet woman, who had struggled so hard to keep her family together after her husband Daniel had died. L.E. stood there by her bedside, that Sunday morning thinking about what a remarkable woman his mother really was. The world really needed more Anice Bennetts. She was the "Book of Knowledge" for all his little questions. She was his comforter, when he felt hurt. She was his strength, at his weakest moments. She was his encourager, whenever he had doubts, but now she was gone, and the pillar that the children once leaned on was now at rest. There was a pain in his throat that he could not move as tears slowly rolled down his cheek. Again he kissed her face and those beautiful hands, and turned and walked away.

## I KISSED THE HAND THAT CRADLED ME

I KISSED THE HAND THAT CRADLED ME,
THAT HELD ME WHILST I SLEPT;
AND SPOKE SOFT WORDS OF COMFORT,
AS DEEP WITHIN I WEPT.
I STOOD THERE BY THE BEDSIDE, HER VOICE
NOW FRAIL AND LOW;
AND LISTENED AS SHE TOLD ME,
TO WEEP FOR HER NO MORE.
I KISSED THE HAND THAT CRADLED ME,
AND WHISPERED IN MY HEART
THOUGH DEATH WOULD TAKE HER FROM ME,
IN MEMORY, WE'D NEVER PART.
I FELT HER FACE, STILL WARM IN DEATH,
AS THERE IN PEACE SHE LAY;
AND VOWED DOWN DEEP WITHIN MY HEART,
WE'D MEET AGAIN SOMEDAY.

L.E. BENNETT, AUGUST 22, 1961

The family gathered at Norcie's house to make funeral arrangements. L.E. was determined that his mother would have a headstone, and the rest of the family agreed. The program was held at Mt. Calvary Baptist Church, with Rev. Langham officiating. Following the service, the family gathered at 1607 Hays Street, where Anice lived, with Mrs. Watkins, a widow. Mack, Carl, Floyd, and L.E. were standing in the front yard talking about the large number of people who attended the funeral. All of Grandma's brothers and sisters, who were alive.

L.E. said, "Isn't it a shame that we have to wait for a funeral like this to get together. We need to start us a family reunion."

The brothers agreed, and on November of 1961 the first Bennett/Parson Family Reunion was held, at Norcie's home in San Antonio. There weren't many in attendance, but L.E. was determined to make it work, so he and Floyd continued the effort. The second reunion was at Brackenridge park in San Antonio, November 1962. July 1963 was the third reunion, at Southside Park. L.E. called Hattie Mae and asked if she would host the Family Reunion at her home, in Louise, Texas. She gleefully accepted. The first reunion was held on July 4, 1964. Hattie worked on the family reunion contacting relatives for a commitment. It became a successful effort, and each year people looked forward to going to Louise. L.E. sent out letters, and the Bennett/Parson Family Reunion flourished. It is held every 3rd Saturday in August, in San Antonio, Texas, now. But, there are future plans to rotate the location.

Well, no rest for the weary. L.E. returned to work and continued his letters to AT&T, and Southwestern Bell management. From the President on down. He also wrote President John F. Kennedy and Robert Kennedy, the Attorney General, as well as Mr. Joseph Bierne, President of the Communication Worker's of America National Union, requesting their assistance in getting the wheels rolling a bit faster in granting equal opportunity to all. Robert Kennedy responded, stating that L.E. was correct concerning the Executive Order and that he should proceed as fore mentioned with his campaign efforts. But to keep a journal and copies of his letters. If

L.E. made absolutely no head way, then the government would step in, and the Executive Order would be enforced. L.E. was pleased to read that bit of support, but really had hoped for a little more. If the telecommunication companies and the CWA wanted to be in compliance with the order, then they needed to make concrete efforts to abide by it. This order and personnel files were L.E.'s stronghold.

D.L. McGowen was the district director for the CWA and his office was located in St. Louis, MO. Mr. Paul Gray was San Antonio's area representative and his office was in Houston. Albert Bowles was the local representative. In 1961 L.E. wrote all of these gentlemen.

D.L. McGowen responded and set up a meeting, to take place in Albert Bowle's office. This was to occur one afternoon during the week.

Mr. McGowen stated that, "he felt integration of the work force would present some very sensitive problems. Black employees working as installers, having to go into the homes of white people. White people who weren't accustomed to having black people come into their homes, that's trouble."

L.E. responded that he had difficulty understanding the logic being used here. When black people had been cooks, housekeepers, yardmen, and now mailmen, they had no trouble going into the homes of white people. What would be so strange about a minority going into a house to install a telephone?

Mr. McGowen's previous statement couldn't be accepted as a reasonable answer. The argument was never settled but L.E. left them with the understanding that the local union wasn't going to stop its quest for equal employment opportunities. Even if it meant having to get the Federal Government involved. AT&T would send representatives to meet with L.E. during the mid to latter part of 1961. The representatives were cordial, and conversation was productive. These people left L.E. with the assurance that they felt AT&T was going to pursue equal opportunities, in accordance with the Executive Order.

Time was of the essence, and it appeared that the union, to

which minorities were paying dues, was stonewalling her minority members, with nothing short of mumbo jumbo. To L.E. time was wasting, and it was too precious to waste. Families were being denied an opportunity to earn respectable wages, commensurate with white employees. The children of these families would be hampered in their quests for a higher education, simply because someone didn't feel they were ready to allow a black person the right opportunity. L.E. would not sit still. He utilized every means at his disposal to push the issue of job opportunities. Meetings were continuing with division level managers, as time moved forward. L.E. was traveling to Harlingen, Brownsville, and Austin, seeking employees who were interested in moving into better paying jobs. There was much receptivity available. He encouraged them to put in letters to request transfers, to watch the bulletin boards for vacancies, and to apply for these jobs by letter format, since minorities weren't given the right to bid as other union white members. Some Mexican Americans had even been allowed to bid, and placed in craft jobs, because they had a lighter complexion. For L.E. these were days of exasperation. First he'd get a glimmer of hope and then nothing would happen. Progress seemed to have been moving so slow.

One night he came home exhausted and stressed. Essie had his dinner waiting for him. The kids would be playing and chattering, as kids do. However, on this particular night L.E. had no patience for noise and demanded total silence. After a few minutes, the chatter and laughter started up again. L.E. yanked his belt off his waist and went to hit each of the kids. Sharon was jumping and flapping so much that the belt wrapped around her arm and flew from L.E.'s hand. Sharon let out a loud squeal. The metal buckle hit her on the left cheek, causing bleeding and a scar. It looked like the shape of Florida turned sideways. L.E. felt broken hearted about this, and Essie was hysterical. Essie cleaned the wound and put a band aid on it. To injure his daughter was certainly not L.E.'s intention.

He would hold that small precious face between his large hands and kiss it, saying, "Baby, Daddy's so sorry, I love you."

Sharon smiled, showing her dimples, and said, "I love you, too,

Daddy."

, L.E. is only human. A human with immense pressures bearing down on his shoulders, as he tried to move his little part of the world. But years would pass before he would put his hands across her face. However, the boys would occasionally endure harsh whippings.

It was time for another car. Not having to deal with the bus and transfers would save time that L.E. could use to rest. So, he purchased a 1955 red and white Ford Fairlane, with white walled tires and shiny hub caps. Now, he was still riding the bus for work, while Essie kept a car for errands and the kids. When Sunday mornings rolled around, if he were off, he would get the family and head to Mt. Calvary Baptist Church. He felt real good about taking his family to church. Sometimes, on Friday nights he would take the family to the Lincoln Drive Inn. They'd order foot long hot dogs and sodas. It was a real nice treat for him and the family, since they spent little leisure time together. With his being in school, homework, local politics, working in the union, and taking care of his regular job, time together was a rare and precious commodity. But he made do the best he could.

You might say L.E. was burning the candle at both ends. But, it was a thrill to him, because he was helping people, and sometimes he even saw results.

He was still meeting with Albert Bowles, Paul Gray, and occasionally having conversations with D.L. McGowen in St. Louis, MO. It was the summer of 1962 when the CWA held their annual meeting in Kansas City, Missouri, at the Muehlbach Hotel. L.E. was looking forward to going to the convention and representing local union #6131. He wrote Joseph Bierne, President of the CWA, and requested a meeting with him during the time of the convention. L.E. and Essie made their travel plans. They were filled with excitement, as they decided to go by train. This would be the least expensive route. They purchased their tickets and made the necessary phone calls to secure accommodations at the Muehlbach Hotel. They were both filled with anticipation. It would be a little get away for them, like a mini vacation. No kids fussing, crying, or throwing food. No meals to prepare, no house to clean. Finally, the day arrived and the children were driven to El Campo, to stay with Essie's parents. L.E. and Essie then drove to Houston where they spent a few hours visiting with his brother, Mack, and his wife Ruby. Essie's brother, Ollie, and his wife Jessie also came over to visit. They had fun catching up with each others lives, and were then taken to the station, where Essie and L.E. caught the train to Kansas City.

L.E. focused his energy on the meeting with Joseph Bierne. He looked forward to their gathering with anticipation, and contemplated the discussions they would have concerning implementation of the Executive Order, and the assistance the National Union Office, could render. Once the train was underway, L.E. discovered there were other CWA members aboard, and he established a pretty good rapport with some of them. They were all white, but very friendly. It was during this train ride, that he met a young red-head caucasian man from Waco, Texas. The two embarked on a great conversation about working for the telephone company. After their impromptu conversation L.E. returned to his meditation on the upcoming encounter with Joseph Bierne. His emotions swirled with the thought of the added fire power that could be applied from the National President. His help could be instrumental in bringing about equality in the company. The train passed through Independence, Mo. The birthplace of Harry S. Truman, who was a president that didn't mind telling it like it was. "Old give em hell, Harry." Soon the train pulled into the station at Kansas City. A cab was hailed and the Bennett's headed for the Muehlbach Hotel. When they arrived at the hotel, and got their room assignment, Essie was looking forward to taking a rest break. But not L.E., "Mr. Curiousity," he couldn't sit still. He went to the lobby and mingled with some of the convention goers. Actually, he went looking for some other black union members. He met one couple, but they didn't really click. They were friendly and cordial, but just didn't have the vitality that L.E. was looking for. He knew there were a lot of black union members, but evidently, their participation was by dues only. He roamed around a little longer then headed back to his room to watch the boob tube.

It was seven p.m. and time for the delegates dinner. Finally, L.E. would come face to face with Joseph Bierne on a personal level, prior to their scheduled meeting. The ballroom was crowded, and beautifully decorated. L.E. and Essie were sharply dressed, in their Sunday's finest. This was their time to rise and shine. L.E. was prepared to make a lasting impression. L.E. gave his name at the door, then he and Essie were escorted to their table. They looked around the room at the large crowd of people, and there was really no one present they recognized. The couple walked around introducing themselves to other delegates and made conversation. Then L.E. saw Albert Bowles, Paul Gray, and D.L. McGowen. L.E. introduced Essie to Albert Bowles, and they chatted for awhile.

Albert then said, "L.E. let me take you over and introduce you to Mr. Bierne, the National President."

At last, the hour had arrived. L.E. was filled with expectations of meeting this gentleman with whom he had only corresponded. Albert led L.E. and Essie over to a group of men, who were standing in a circle talking and laughing. Albert touched one of the gentlemen on the back. When the man turned around, L.E. immediately recognized him from a CWA photo.

Albert said, "Mr. Bierne, I would like you to meet L.E. Bennett, President of Local #6131, in San Antonio, Texas."

L.E. smiled and extended his hand to shake Mr. Bierne's. But, Mr. Bierne stood there with a straight face, looking L.E. in the eye. Bierne said, "We've corresponded." He then turned his back to L.E. and continued his conversation with the other fellows in his circle.

L.E. was so infuriated, that he almost burst into cursing, right there in the ballroom. How embarrassing and humiliating to be snubbed as though he were nothing. However, kicking this man's butt right here in this ballroom wouldn't help his cause. Essie gently grabbed his hand, and L.E. managed to contain himself.

He thought, fine, we'll definitely take this up tomorrow at our scheduled meeting. He fully intended to tell Bierne exactly how he felt.

"That I'm paying my hard earned money, which is used to help pay your salary. As far as I'm concerned, you are a sorry son of a gun. You may be great in the eyes of others, but I just lost respect for you."

The next day, Joe Bierne never showed for the scheduled meeting. He sent his executive vice president, Glenn Watts, instead, which added insult to injury. L.E. felt that what Bierne had done was totally and completely unreasonable. It was hard for L.E. to imagine that someone you were paying to represent your best interest could behave with such blatant disrespect. From then on it was one day at a time dealing with controlling his anger. He and Bierne never directly spoke or corresponded again. However, all was not lost, the second day after their arrival, convention day was finally here. There would be microphones spread throughout the convention floor, allowing union delegates to stand, and once recognized, they could speak. This would be L.E.'s opportunity. He approached a microphone and patiently waited his turn. All the delegates, representatives, and directors were there, including J. Bierne. L.E. thought to himself that when his turn came, he would greet everyone, and then proceed to tell the convention and Bierne exactly how he felt and what was expected of his union leaders. L.E. would state that his local #6131 minority members, as well as others were paying the same membership dues and they deserved the same union representation.

Minorities should be allowed to bid for craft jobs and they should be supported by their union to which they've paid dues. Looking Bierne, the man who disrespected him, in the eyes, L.E. would say, "It's a sorry day in hell when a union has a president that gladly takes your money into his pockets, but acts as though you don't exist. Maybe, this union needs a different president. One that will represent all of her members not just some. Like it or not the President of the United States signed an Executive Order, stating that any company doing business with the Federal Government was going to have to abide by it. It's a new day. We want change and we want it now."

But, L.E. was never recognized. He was never able to verbalize at that convention all of his thoughts and feelings. He wondered, if that was a deliberate act. Was it because of all the agitation he'd been doing to have blacks promoted? He would never know, but it would never hinder his ambitions.

As the convention weekend drew to a close, plans were made to return home. Their train was scheduled to leave around midnight. While they were packing, a rap came at the door. At the door was the young white red-haired gentleman from the train. Mr. C. told L.E. that some hotheads were down in the bar, and they were talking about teaching L.E. a lesson for that mouth of his. They were planning to do harm to him and his wife for what he was trying to accomplish. Mr. C. further expressed that maybe L.E. and Essie should leave early, because when people are drinking, they can do some crazy things. He just thought L.E. should know what was brewing. L.E. thanked him and closed the door. He stood there leaning against the door and looking at Essie, still in the bedroom packing. He decided not to tell her of the impending danger. He did know that if anyone tried to harm his wife, they would have to kill him. L.E. had always been considered a time freak. He looked at his watch and realized they had a few hours before they were due at the station. He went into the bedroom and asked Essie if she'd like to see a movie instead of sitting around the room? She agreed and checked the newspaper. There was a theatre near the hotel showing, "Adrain's Messenger" at eight p.m. Neither one of them knew anything about the movie, but decided to give it a try. It didn't start for another half hour, but the longer L.E. sat there the angrier he became.

He thought to himself, "This is the kind of shit that makes you want to kill somebody." He told Essie, "Let's get our bags and get the hell out of here; and nobody had better say a word to me, unless it's goodbye."

Essie thought nothing of his mood, since she had witnessed the events of the convention. It was understandable.

They went to the desk and checked out without incident. Then they walked to the front of the hotel, and hailed a cab to the movie house. They watched all the previews of coming attractions and the movie. L.E. and Essie then took a cab to the train station. Their wait was not very long before boarding began, and they received their seat assignments. They were safely on the train and headed home. Looking out the window as the train began to pull off, L.E. thought about the warning of impending peril and how wasteful it was for individuals to spend energy trying to deter the progress that others so rightfully deserved. Huh, typical, L.E. thought. He became more determined to finish what he started.

The train had been underway for a while, when Mr. C. came to L.E.'s seat.

"L.E., man I'm sure glad to see that you all made it out alright. They were banging on your hotel room door and looking around for you." Again, L.E. thanked him for his concern. They never saw each other again after that. Every now and then, Mr. C. would cross L.E.'s mind, and he would wonder what happened to him. L.E. hoped he has a good life. He would certainly always be grateful for the friendship that he extended at that time in his life. The Bennett's made it back to Houston without further incident, picked up their car , and headed for El Campo. They were glad to see the children. They spent a couple of days with Essie's parents and listening to the kids stories of their days on the farm. The children really loved spending time with their grandparents and cousins. They would feed the chickens, slop the hogs, play stick ball, and take turns laying with Granddad Dave in the hammock, looking up at the stars. He was always so patient with them. Now, he is one of the stars.

## KNOW, LISTEN, REMEMBER

### KNOW WHEN TO STAND YOUR GROUND
### KNOW WHEN TO HOLD STILL
KNOW WHEN TO FORGE AHEAD

LEARN WHEN TO SPEAK
LEARN WHEN TO LISTEN
LEARN ALL YOU CAN FROM EVERYONE

REMEMBER A TRUE CHRISTIAN HATES NO ONE
IS COMPASSIONATE, AND
APPLAUDES YOUR SUCCESS,
RATHER THAN BE ENVIOUS

SHARON BENNETT-WILLIAMS

# CHAPTER IX

L. E. was in a pensive mood on the drive back to San Antonio. He wondered, what in the world could have gone wrong with the hopes and dreams for a successful meeting. The anticipated help that he thought would be forthcoming, to deal with the process of moving house-service people to better paying jobs. His resolve strengthened. He's Dan Bennett's son, and he refused to let any stumbling blocks stand in his way. He was more determined than ever to continue his mission and achieve the goals of affirmative action with the implementation of J. F. K.'s Executive Order. Progress will come if they just continue to ardently defend their position. Due to a lack of activity from Mr. Haywood, in the traffic division, L.E. decided to use some outside intervention. In the fall of 1962, he contacted Mr. Eugene Coleman of the SNAP newspaper of San Antonio, and asked for his assistance in the unions efforts. This was a local black owned and operated paper, that was willing to give some publicity to the unions plight.

Mr. Coleman suggested that L.E. speak with Dr. Ruth Bellinger and get the local National Association for the Advancement of Colored People (NAACP) involved. Yes, the sister of the woman they purchased their home from, on Ervin Street. L.E. and Mr. Coleman met with Dr. Bellinger and she readily agreed to lend their assistance. L.E. would continue to address the problem from the inside, and Dr. Bellinger along with the local NAACP would pursue the problem from the outside. Now, L.E. became a member of the NAACP and attended their meetings to discuss strategies. The NAACP began by making phone calls to key telephone company management, and followed up with letters. Dr. Bellinger also attended some of the company meetings with L.E.

The division plant manager had turned his meeting with local #6131 over to the division plant personnel supervisor, Harper Nations. Mr. Nations had proven to be a man one could talk to, but not really expect a whole lot from. After all, his duty was to protect the company and its status quo. L.E. was trying to fight the good fight for those who were afraid that they would lose their jobs, if they pressed too hard. These people had been used to receiving nothing, now they were facing something new, they were scared. Most of the white employees would whisper and glare, but rarely did anyone speak out against what the black union members were trying to achieve. On the one hand the white employees understood about a person wanting better things in life; on the other hand they feared losing what was theirs.

L.E. told Harper Nations that, " The company shouldn't only consider San Antonio based jobs for advancement, but any jobs within the district. The local #6131 would be glad to review job opportunities anywhere in south Texas."

L.E. further stated that, "If there was an opening, and no one else would take the job, then he would take it, rather than see the job go unfilled by a black union member." L.E. thought about that statement many times afterward, but he never recanted, because he meant it. L.E. firmly believed that you cannot lead where you are not willing to go, even if it's sometimes undesirable. How can you, as a leader, send others where you yourself are not willing to go. As things progressed, it would not be too much longer before L.E. would have the opportunity to stand behind his words.

Not every black employee was interested in being in the open about their desires to move into a better position. Many elder members were still concerned about problems on the job with white employees. They wanted the glory without the sacrifice. There were also some who were playing both ends against the middle. These employees were of the mind to let the union work for them, but they were not going to involve themselves in the union. If the axe falls, it will get those who are out front, and they'll be spared. People of that mentality were few in number, nevertheless, they presented a negative idea that the public lingered on; that black people were satisfied with minimum wages and non-skilled work.

The battle went on and the pace kept up, with politics playing a major role. L.E.'s grades were beginning to reflect the wear and tear on him, both mentally and physically. During the summer of 1963, L.E. was admitted to the hospital by Dr. Stanley Stain. The diagnosis was exhaustion and dehydration. He was placed on a regimen of medication and rest. The doctor wanted him to only rest, until he saw some improvement in L.E.'s physical condition. After only one day in the hospital, L.E. had his wife bring him "Ole Faithful", his black Underwood typewriter along with his school books and union books. L.E. was having a ball typing letters, when Dr. Stain made his rounds. When the doctor entered the room and found L.E. sitting in the middle of the bed with his typewriter, and papers everywhere, he threw the papers off the bed.

He shouted harshly, "I told you I wanted you to rest. How in the world do you think you're going to recuperate, if you continue to do the same things you were doing at home? Call your wife, and have her come pick up all this stuff. Don't let me make rounds again and find this stuff still here. I want you resting and getting well." The doctor then stormed out of the room. Essie already due to come visit that evening with the kids, took the materials home. From that day forward, L.E. followed the doctors orders.

Once released from the hospital, it was back to the old grindstone, but L.E. felt rejuvenated. Rest was just what he needed. Seems like there was always some candidate to support for congress or as judge. Albert Pena, Henry Gonzales, Johnny Alaniz, and Rudy Esquivel just to name a few. It kept him going, attending one function after another. There were state conventions and meetings with the telephone company. His efforts were beginning to come into reality, and victory seemed to be just around the corner. August of 1963 the phone company had conceded to the union demands and allowed black employees to bid on craft jobs. They were to also list these craft positions as available for new applicants. A few weeks later, L.E. received calls concerning possible jobs available in Victoria, Texas and elsewhere. Nobody was too interested in leaving San Antonio and no blacks had been placed in craft positions, yet. Albert Bowles, the CWA representative, kept in touch, and feelings were beginning to mount within L.E. that something positive was ready to happen. The march on Washington was shaping up, and there was plenty of talk on T.V., as well as, in the papers about the impending event. The atmosphere was thick with excitement and aspirations. The NAACP, CORE (Congress of Racial Equality), SCLC (Southern Christian Leadership Conference), and others were pushing the right buttons, it seemed. The walls were beginning to crack. L.E. felt like the time was now, for black Americans to elevate. Companies couldn't continue to deny upward movement for their minority employees.

It was August 1963, L.E. worked out of the Diamond Central Office now, and he had acquired an old 1949 black Dodge four door. They now had two vehicles. Despite his circumstances, they were a two car family. Of course, L.E. drove the old Dodge and Essie drove the Ford Fairlane. You couldn't hardly pry her hands off the steering wheel. Now, she could run errands whenever she needed to, without calling someone for a ride. The family also purchased a three bedroom, one bath, one car garage, brick home with a fenced yard, on Monterey street, on the city's west side. It was a nice new spacious home with the hardwood floors, Essie loved.

On August 28, 1963, L.E. heard Dr. King give his infamous "I have a Dream" speech. Watching it on television, he became exhilarated. It was like taking a drink of premium pink champagne. It was a powerful tonic drink. This man vocalized the hopes and dreams of so many Black people. This day, a hero rose higher in L.E.'s sight, and all his hopes and dreams were mirrored in that one speech. "I have a dream that one day _____." You can fill in the blank, because each of us has our own dream. We are each striving to achieve something that we feel will be meaningful in our lives, and the lives of others.

Yes, there would be those who would attempt to stand in L.E.'s way, but every chance he got, he stood and spoke his peace. All of L.E.'s life he was the one who would stand up for the underdog. It was something that he inherited from Daniel and Anice Bennett. Someone has to speak for the underdog. L.E. left the office at the end of the day, after watching M.L.K., ecstatic, exhilarated, impassioned, and on fire. When he arrived home, his next door neighbor, Carl Tyson, was out working in the yard. The two men talked for quite a while about Dr. Kings' speech.

Carl said, "Man! That fellow is going to be president one day."

Of course, L.E. agreed. Ultimately, their conversation ended, and L.E. went into the house.

Essie and the children greeted him, and they all prepared for dinner. There was great conversation at the dinner table, mostly about the speech. L.E. and Essie always encouraged the children to participate in conversation, at the table. They felt this would enlighten the children and make them smarter, stronger, and more successful adults, and better able to function in life and not be afraid to speak up. Sharon learned this lesson, well.

The company wasn't giving any real open hints or clues as to what specific strategy or time table they would take. Management's focus was if someone was to be promoted, they had to be in good standing in their current position. This was an understandable position. No one had any difficulty comprehending that. The union wanted good representation, as well. The company had to protect their position with all of the local unions. L.E. had the feeling that the company would do what it had to do, in maintaining credibility with all of the unions. When time came to move a minority to a craft job, it would then be demonstrated that they kept their end of the bargain, of abiding by the order, that required equal opportunity employment for all, by seeking qualified people. No one was interested in tokenism, the union wanted a real equal opportunity for all its qualified employees.

The country had now progressed through August on a wane of great feelings of elation and possibilities, with the glowing speech by Dr. King still ringing on their ears. L.E. still worked at the Diamond Central Office, on November 22, 1963, a day he will never forget. It burned bright in his mind. Probably, no living American would ever forget that date. The young President of the United States stopped in San Antonio to pick up Lyndon B. Johnson, and then headed to Carswell Airforce Base, outside of Dallas, Texas for a very important speech.

Everyone was buzzing about the President coming through San Antonio, again. Many were looking forward to watching his speech on television.

L.E. and Melvin Porter were just returning to the office following lunch. L.E. went to the second floor to check building conditions. Entering the test center, he saw men sitting silently in their test positions, and women with tear stained faces. The voice of Walter Cronkite emanated from the television stating something to the effect of, "Ladies and Gentlemen, I am sorry to report, the President of the United States is dead." L.E. was stupefied. His body went numb, and he stood dumb founded. He then asked one of the women, what happened? She replied that President Kennedy had been shot in Dallas and he died. L.E.. turned around with tears in his eyes, and walked slowly back down the stairs to the basement. He couldn't believe what he heard. He then went out the back way and walked around for awhile. Why would someone want to kill J.F.K.?

L.E. just kept saying to himself, "The President is dead, the President is dead." It almost seemed like a bad dream, and hopefully, he would awaken to find that all was well, and Kennedy was still alive. However, reality soon set in, and he knew that the man he respected and admired was truly dead. The era known as "Camelot" came to a close. There was something about John Kennedy that captured L.E.'s imagination. He was a young and eloquent speaker, who believed in the youth of this country and their future.

What would this mean to the effort that L.E. was putting forth at the company? Would they make his job more difficulty for trying to bring about equal employment? Would there be more assassinations? Besides, Martin Luther King had been loudly speaking of equal rights since the mid-fifties. Medgar Evers had been gunned down, as well. Robert Kennedy was of the same frame of mind as his brother. Does this mean something is brewing? Would our lives and livelihood be lost? L.E. resolved within his mind, that these were issues he could do nothing about. We would just have to wait and see, what time had to offer.

That weekend was a total waste for L.E. as he spent most of it watching television. He couldn't remember what the pastor preached on that Sunday, as he and the family sat in the pew. Getting back to the television, and listening to the radio during the interim was most important. As he and the family left church, the car atmosphere was one of melancholy. J.F.K. was dead and the future appeared bleak. The country must move on from this point, and make the best out of what we have. But, there was this nagging thought of apprehension in the back of L.E.'s mind, about Lyndon B. Johnson having been sworn in as the next president. What can minorities expect, in the way of Civil Rights, from President Johnson? The thought about how smoothly the transition had taken place, ran through L.E.'s mind. Johnson flew with Kennedy into Dallas as Vice President, but he left Dallas on Air Force one as President, without an injury. What a magnificent document our constitution is. Would Johnson really honor what J.F.K. had started? How strong will he stand behind the growing Civil Rights effort? L.B. Johnson had been a U.S. senator from Texas, but L.E. wasn't up to speed on Johnson's civil right's position. Time would tell just how effectively he would implement civil rights laws, to help bring about the changes in the work place throughout the nation that were so needed.

News reports continued on the assassination of John F. Kennedy by Lee Harvey Oswald. They tried to piece together just what had happened on that fateful Friday in Dallas, Texas. All kinds of scenarios were imagined as to who, what, and why? The pain of losing a friend and advocate in such a high place was deep. The funeral procession, with the horse drawn carriage carrying the bier of the

fallen president, was watched by millions on TV. L.E. has fervent
memories of little John-John standing and saluting the cortege as it
passed in review. As his father, the slain president, was carried to his
final earthly resting place at Arlington Cemetery. It caused a lump in
L.E.'s throat. He sat there watching intently.

Seeing John-John reminded him of how he had stood by the
bedside, where his own father had lay. He then pulled back the
pure and white sheet, and L.E. looked at the handsome face of his
deceased father. He was not too much older than John-John, when
Dan died. It was hard for L.E. to hold back the tears, as he watched
the ceremony. He commiserated with that little boy, and wondered
how life would be for him growing up without his father. Would
Jacqueline Kennedy be as strong a mother to John-John as Anice
Bennett was to him? L.E. mused on that thought briefly, and thought
to himself, each of us has a cross to bear, while living in this world.
John-John will make it, just as so many others have done. Time told
us that Jacqueline was a wonderful mother, and still our queen of
Camelot until her own death. (John Kennedy, Jr. died in a plane crash
July 16, 1999)


## GIVE US STRENGTH O'LORD

ON BENDED KNEES WE SHOULD PRAY
FOR OUR FAMILY AND FRIENDS,
ON EARTH AND THE HEAVENS ABOVE.
ASK THE LORD TO GIVE YOU COMFORT,
AND SPIRITUAL STRENGTH,
TO MAKE IT THROUGH ANOTHER DAY.
YOU'VE LOST A LOVED ONE,
AND IT HURTS DEEP WITHIN;
BUT, FEAR NOT!
IF, YOUR FAMILY HAS ROOTED YOU IN LOVE,
AND YOU'VE ALLOWED GOD TO BLANKET
YOU IN HIS SPIRIT,

**THEN THE PAIN WILL PASS, AND
BE REPLACED WITH THE JOY OF HIS LOVE!
WE SHALL MEET AGAIN!**

**<u>SHARON BENNETT-WILLIAMS (2001)</u>**

# CHAPTER X

It was the spring of 1964, when the unions aspirations were finally realized. L.E. still worked at the Diamond Central Office, when Harper Nations, the Division Plant Personnel Supervisor asked to meet with him for lunch.

Mr. Nations came over to pick L.E. up and they went to the San Antonio International Airport to have lunch. As they ate their meal, Harper informed L.E. that two craft positions were definitely available in Corpus Christi, Texas, for two linemen. He further explained that a candidate had been found for one of the positions, but they've yet to find someone for the second. Harper reminded L.E. that he'd once made the statement, "If you can't find anybody to fill a position, then as a last resort, I will go, just be sure one of my black union members gets the opportunity."

L.E. remembered having made such a statement. Now, it was put up, or shut up time. L.E. inquired as to who the other candidate was, that accepted the first slot? It was Lawrence Randle, his vice president in Local Union #6131. L.E. then asked Mr. Nations, if he had exhausted the listed applicants, for whom L.E. had typed letters requesting consideration for craft job upgrades? Harper assured L.E. that they've all been contacted, and Randle was the only one who had accepted. However, James Charleston was thinking about it, but didn't really think he'd go. Mr. Nations expressed to L.E. that if he was unable to get anyone else from his union, then they would have to fill the position via other means.

Back at work L.E. contacted James Charleston to inquire if he was seriously interested, and could he give the union a decision.

Mr. Charleston indicated that he had too many things standing in his way, and that he would not be able to take that position. The next person L.E. called was Lawrence Randle, to confirm that he was actually going to accept the position. Randle informed him that he fully intended to go to Corpus Christi. L.E. continued calling his other union members seeking someone to take this opportunity. If he could not find anyone else to fill this position, then he would have to drop out of school, and go to avoid the position going to a non-minority. Also, so that Randle would not be alone.

His efforts to find someone else were unsuccessful, but he didn't want to readily accept the position; because someone may come along and say that the union officers weren't doing all that work to get its members promoted, but only so they could get themselves a better job. Of course, the officers wanted better paying jobs just like those they represented. But, it was only a half-true statement. L.E.'s main concern was that the others were taken care of first, before he considered himself. L.E. could not tolerate the thought of someone saying he was just looking out for number one. So, he tried diligently to get another person to accept this position. No one was interested in going to Corpus. After all the complaints and letters requesting better jobs, no one was willing to make the ultimate sacrifice and relocate. Most had just purchased homes, or had them built, and they weren't thinking of moving out of San Antonio. As a matter of fact, L.E. and Essie Lee had only been in their brand new home a little more than a year. They had not even gotten the newness worn off of the house.

After a relentless search, L.E. concluded that he would have to be a man of his word, and take the position. It was now reality. He will have to leave school, sell their brand new home, while uprooting his wife and children from familiar surroundings and friends. His statement had come back to bite him. But, like his father, he would stand behind his word. He remembered his mother telling him about the type of man Dan Bennett was, and how he never told anybody he was going to do something, and then to not do it. Dan always kept his word. Now it was L.E.'s time to keep his word.

L.E. knew how difficult this would be for Essie. She loved that house. It had some of the features that she always wanted, and besides, this was her first new home. A home that no one else had lived in before. She was the one to break it in, and have things just as she wanted them. He thought about the situation all the way home that evening. How best to convince her, that he had to do what a man had to do. He really needed her support. L.E. hoped she would realize what it meant to keep his word, and that he was giving up something, as well. Disrupting her happy home life, leaving a house she picked out herself. The pain of seeing his children uprooted, moved to a strange location, and having to make new friends. Starting all over again from scratch. Try as he may, he could not think of a good way to tell Essie. Her response was of the utmost importance to him. This was a woman, that the Lord had given him as his wife, and disappointing her was the last thing in the world he wanted to do. How could he make this seem plausible to her? What magic phrase could he use, that would put her on the same side of the fence that he now found himself.

His long slow drive home came to an end. L.E. had to face the music. At least, Essie knew and liked Dorothy Randle very much, Lawrence's wife. Essie could call her and they could commiserate together. That was one plus, but beyond that he saw no glimmer of hope. Essie met him at the door, and the children were in the backyard playing. L.E. hugged and kissed her hello.

He stood there holding her in his arms, looking into her eyes, and said, "Honey, lets sit down, I need to tell you something." They took a seat on the couch, and he paused for a while. L.E. then began to unravel the story, about all the work that he had been doing to get minorities better jobs, the statement he made, and the recent position offer.

Essie looked at him and kind of put a small smile on her face, perhaps, to hide the tears in her heart. "Daddy, can't you tell them, you were just joking, that you really didn't mean it, she asked?" (She called him Daddy, because the children called him whatever she called him. For a while the kids were calling him L.E.)

She was deeply saddened by the news, but she was always a loyal supporter of her husband, and when all was said and done, the bottom line was she would stand with her husband. He knew he could count on her, but how to assuage the pain? She began to ask questions about Corpus Christi. What is Corpus like? Who do you know down there? How is the housing? How are the schools? L.E. and Essie further discussed options on what to do with their current home.

After what seemed like a thousand questions and statements, Essie said, "Daddy, I sure will hate leaving my home, but honey, if this is what you must do, I think you already know that I'm with you."

Those were some of the sweetest words he's heard, since the day he asked her to marry him. This was music to his ears because he'd always relied on her strong fervent support.

Now was the time for setting things in order. L.E. and Randle were to report to Glen Smith, in Corpus Christi, May of 1964. Randle was more familiar with Corpus than L.E., because his father had a piece of property on the coast. Randle was accustomed to going down there to fish, and fool around during the summer months. L.E. had an Aunt, by the name of Gladys Brown, who had lived in Corpus for all of her adult life. Gladys was tall, firmly built, brown-skinned, with glasses. This was the youngest sister on his mother's side of the family. Gladys was a friendly, outgoing person, who had no problems showing the family around town.

May rolled around and marching orders were received, and temporary living arrangements were made for the men, at a motel on Shoreline Boulevard. The families packed and made preparations to follow soon. Meanwhile, in San Antonio others were moved into craft jobs of installation and construction. The gate had been opened in the plant department, but there was still work to be done in the other departments, such as telephone operators. The NAACP was involved with continuing the push for telephone operators, and L.E. felt confident that the effort would continue in his absence.

Now, after eight years of faithful employment and striving to acquire civil rights for minorities, he and Lawrence Randle were the first black linemen in this area for Southwestern Bell. How sweet the taste in his mouth, of climbing that mountain and making that successful gain. It would be 1968 when the first African-American telephone operators were hired, with the NAACP leading the way.

L.E. and Randle arrived in Corpus Christi over the weekend, checked into the motel on Shoreline Blvd., and made ready to report to work that Monday morning. The motel location was beautiful, overlooking the Gulf Coast. But, it was just a preface to a possibly ugly encounter. L.E. envisioned a sea of white angry faces confronting them on Monday. Would these individuals make their lives hard just because they were black; or would they be agreeable, and willing to help teach the newcomers the ropes? L.E. thought about how he couldn't tolerate the idea of letting Randle go alone. He figured it would be harder to break two men than one. They would have each other to support and commiserate with. L.E. remembered how invaluable Ulysses Axiel was when they were fighting the battle for equal opportunity. Practically, everywhere L.E. went, Axiel went with him, because he felt that L.E. needed a safety valve to let off steam. Axiel's age and experience were invaluable to L.E. in the many meetings they attended. The two rode the highway between San Antonio and Houston numerous times, attending one meeting after another. Because of this, He realized it would be a mistake to let Randle make the journey alone. Now, they will be able to help each other at the end of a hard day. People were making a change that they really didn't want to make, support would be valuable to their success.

Monday morning came and the two new black linemen arrived bright and early at seven thirty a.m. for their eight a.m. shift. They met their construction foreman, Glen (Smitty) Smith, at the company storeroom, on Caranchau Street. Glen was polite, and courteous, but somewhat standoffish. He didn't give anybody the impression, that he was their friend, just their supervisor. Mr. Smith led the two around and introduced them to the men in the line gang. Nobody seemed overly receptive to L.E. and Randle's arrival. Afterward, they were each assigned a preceptor with whom they would be indoctrinated to their duties. L.E.'s preceptor was George Treff, and Randle was assigned to work with Eddie. There was a distinct feeling of resentment in the group, but nothing overt. What else would they expect of the group? Certainly, not someone running out to greet them with a big bear hug. But, the ice had been broken, and like it or not, they would have to work together.

Glen Smith was a real slender, bespectacled man, in his mid to late fifties. He often referred to a person as laddie. Glen knew his job and was emphatic about everyone learning theirs. He gave men the impression that he would not accept excuses, he wanted results. The days came and went, and there were days when L.E.'s coworkers got on his nerves. L.E. and Randle sometimes left the storeroom at the close of day, leaving a set of three tracks behind them. Two feet, and their butt dragging on the ground, from the exhaustion of the day.

Hurricane Celia had just gone through Corpus, and a lot of damage was done. The work was hard. It was nothing short of slave labor, L.E. thought. It could be harsh, because they had been used to working inside air conditioned buildings. Now they were working outside in the hot humid weather trying to get the telephone poles and cables back into shape. It was back breaking work. Each day presented many new challenges. Time was slow and hard. Glen never gave the impression that he cared more about one laddie than another. He expected the experienced men to show the greenhorns about what it meant to be in a line gang. The work was dirty and hard, but gratifying, because each day they learned something new, and they could see the fruits of their labor. By evening, they had something new to talk about. There were days when the preceptors would have high praise for what was achieved, and it would serve to stifle the anger. But, make no mistake about it, there were days when L.E. and Randle felt like killing somebody. However, they knew that wasn't the reason they accepted the challenge, to be the first black linemen in Corpus Christi. No, they were there to work, to be as successful as possible. Because when the dirty work was finished, they knew there would be something better up the road. If they couldn't make it as linemen, then it would be a blown opportunity, because who is to say there would be a second chance.

At the end of the day he and Randle would go by Mom's Cafè, which was owned by a distant relative of L.E.'s. Mom was a sweet and endearing lady who served really good food. It represented the closest thing to home cooking. She fixed them dinner, and prepared their lunch for the next day.

One Sunday, when they were having dinner at Mom's, they heard a gunshot. Pretty soon, the police came with their sirens screeching, and then an ambulance. A gentleman ran in the café and sat down at a table. The man began talking about having to kill someone, because the man had tried to take his money, and he just couldn't allow that. L.E. and Randle can't remember what the man looked like, they just got up and got out of there in a hurry. There was going to be trouble.

L.E. was on the job a year and had reached the point where the sight of George Treff literally made him sick to his stomach. This man hovered over him like a vulture. He inspected and peered at every little detail, even after a year. Things had to be exact and precise. L.E. finally realized the job wasn't about George Treff, it was about the success or failure of L.E. Bennett. Despite how he grew to feel about Treff, the man was doing what he was paid to do, and he knew his job well. L.E. decided to take a negative and turn it into a positive. Though, at times Treff's attitude was pugnacious and nasty, he was still a damn good lineman. So, the advantage to L.E. of working with Treff was to learn as much as he could about being a good lineman, and Treff was going to teach him. He made sure to cross every "T", and dot every "I". This gave him confidence, and whenever Glen came behind him to check on his work, L.E. didn't have to worry about it. It seemed like it was just in his blood to do it right, and L.E. came to rely on that.

After a month or so, L.E. rented a house at 2509 Koepke Street, right across from Crossley Elementary School. This would prove to be very convenient for the children. It was a nice house, with beautiful hardwood floors, three bedrooms, two bathrooms, and a detached garage. Essie loved those floors, and the neighborhood. The next door neighbors were Felmon and Bertha Barnes, who were sterling people with children of their own. It was close to Aunt Gladys, as well. These were some of the most helpful people one would want to meet. Essie and the children joined L.E. June of 1964.

Essie found employment at Spohn Hospital as a nurse's aid, in the nursery, on the eleven p.m. to seven a.m. shift. To help bring extra income into the house. It also meant that L.E. had to fix Sharon's hair for school. He wasn't very good at it, but he did his best. Sharon learned quickly how to do her own hair. She missed the French braided angel rings her mother put on the top of her head. But, Essie made up for it, by doing the angel ring on her off days. However, working nights was extremely difficult for Essie, especially when she couldn't get eight hours of sleep during the day. She chose this shift after discovering Kenneth was being abused by the sitter, and he had two to three years to go before he could start school. Essie then went to work at the Central Kitchen for the Corpus Independent School District. She worked there until she discovered she was with child, in 1966. During the middle of Essie's pregnancy, she went to work at Memorial Hospital.

The Bennett's had to travel to Houston in March of 1966, due to what was described as flu like illness of L.E.'s brother, Mack. However, they discovered that Mack's situation would worsen and lead to his death. His home going service was October of 1966.

It was during this trip back to Houston, that Essie, Martha, Norcie, and Janie would discover that they were all expecting, around the same time. Norcie gave birth to Darrell, Martha bore Audrey, Janie delivered Greta Legayle, and Essie had a big eyed beautiful girl on January 14, 1967, named Lisa Elizabeth. Lisa was a daddy's child from the very start. As soon as she started to walk, she wanted to go everywhere that her Daddy went. In those days, there weren't seatbelts in the cars. So, L.E. would put her behind his shoulder, as she stood up in the front seat. He could use his shoulder to keep her against the seat, that way any time he made a quick stop, he could protect her. Any given day, you just might have seen L.E. and Lisa riding around town, with her standing behind his shoulder. Today we know that's not the way to travel, and thank goodness we have seatbelts.

June of 1967, the young Bennett family purchased a home at 234 Westgate, which was close to Miller High School and the Buccaneer Stadium. This was in walking distance, and the family attended many Miller Buccaneer football games. On his off weekends, L.E. would take Louis, Sharon, and Kenneth down to the "T" heads, which was on Shoreline Drive, along the coast. Kenneth would ride on his skateboard, Louis would play with his model airplanes, and Sharon would roller skate. The kids all had their favorites, and L.E. and Essie tried to appease them, whenever possible. Louis liked yellow cake, vanilla ice cream, orange soda, and Elvis Presley. Don't ask. Sharon loved strawberry shortcake, strawberry ice cream, Red soda, and the Tempting Temptations. Kenneth was wild about chocolate cake, chocolate ice cream, root beer soda, and James Brown. L.E. brought each of them their first record albums of their favorite artist, and when the entertainers came to town, he took them to the concerts.

By this time, L.E. had graduated from working with George Treff, and had been assigned to a truck, in order to work jobs by himself. Between 1964 and 1967, L.E. had gone through a number of job assignments. But it was while he was a lineman, that he had bid on a cable splicers job. One day Glen Smith visited him on the job site. Smitty walked up to the base of the pole, where L.E. was working, and said, "Lad, come down, I need to talk with you." L.E. secured his equipment and began his descent. Once L.E. reached the bottom of the pole, Smitty had already returned to his vehicle. L.E. walked over and sat in the vehicle, and Smitty informed him that he had been accepted on his bid. Glen Smitty Smith gave L.E. the particulars on reporting to his new job assignment.

L.E. thanked him and stated, "Maybe, I might have an occasion to work for you again, who knows."

Smitty said to L.E., "No lad, you won't ever be working for me again. If anything, I may wind up working for you, one day. When you leave here, I just feel that you are going onward and upward. I wish you the best." With that, Smitty shook L.E.'s hand and thanked him for the great job he'd done, then he left.

L.E. stood there at the base of his pole, and reminisced on what he had gone through, and just what the future would hold for him. This first assignment had been quite an experience. Being a lineman was no small achievement. Randle had already been successful on his earlier bid, as well, and had relocated his family back to San Antonio.

L.E. was to report to Ed Janota, his new foreman in the cable splicing crew. Ed Janota had become a supervisor not long ago, himself. L.E. was paired with Richard Trujillo, and found his friendship, as well as his ability as a craftsman, to be superb. The two men worked the cable that was being laid along Padre Island Drive, and Janota was determined to meet his deadlines. His wanting to do a good job was understandable. However, one night, when L.E. and Richard were working in a manhole. Ed showed up and expressed his opinion. He felt that L.E. and Richard could be moving a little faster. One word led to another until they were in a verbal altercation. After he and L.E. finished discussing the matter, work resumed.

Cable splicing was good work, and L.E. enjoyed the experience he was gaining. Things were going quite well, until one day, in the winter of 1965. L.E. was cutting in a new terminal off of Padre Island Drive, close to the Wyman office. It was extremely cold that day. He had swung up his platform, and tied it off. He went up the pole to erect his tent, for protection from the intense cold. L.E.'s hands were so cold, that he could hardly splice the cable pairs. The wind was coming underneath that tent, and it felt icy cold. This was the day L.E. decided that outside work was for the birds. He knew there had to be a better way to earn a living, than just freezing your buns off. He decided to seek an inside job, where it was warm. L.E. placed a request for a Central Office frame job, and was accepted.

L.E. went to work under the supervision of Jim Gilbert, at the Terminal Office. Jerry Darden, Ernest Camiel, and Robert Gunnels were his other co-workers, and the chemistry within the group was real good. Gilbert, sent L.E. to the Wyman Office, which was an Electronic Switching System (ESS). There he would be working with a gentleman by the name of Green. Green took great pains to teach L.E. the ropes. It was exciting, enjoyable work, and it helped increase his overall knowledge of how the circuitry worked in the two different offices. Just he and Green worked that office, therefore, parking was not a problem, and they would take turns driving to coffee breaks. L.E. had not drunk coffee since he first tried it while in basic training, so he drank soda. One May day in 1966 L.E. had parked his car right at the back door, and the door only had one small window to look out through. As they prepared to leave for coffee, they looked through that small back door window and noticed that it was raining cats and dogs, so they decided to wait until it subsided. Once it stopped, they opened the back door, and it was obvious that it had only rained on L.E.'s car.

Green said, "Man, I just don't know whether I want to ride with you or not. It only rained on your car, and nowhere else on the lot."

They looked at each other, and had a really good laugh about the situation. The gentlemen finished their coffee break and prepared to head back to the office.

Green said, "Maybe we had better look and see if it rained on your car again. If it has, man, I'm calling me a cab."

They concluded that it probably was the result of a water spout from the Gulf. Who knows?

After much trial and effort to get other African Americans promoted, L.E. finally was on his way and there was no stopping him now. He attended and passed the San Antonio Area Assessment Center for Management, in 1968. In the fall of 1969, L.E. would become the first African-American management employee (frame-foreman), in the San Antonio area, which covered San Antonio to El Paso (east to west); and Amarillo to Brownsville (north to south). He was then moved to a position as first line supervisor in the Special Services District. From there L.E. earned a promotion to Toll Methods Supervisor in Plant Operations at General Headquarters, in St. Louis, Missouri; with oversight responsibility for the special services operation for Southwestern Bell Company. This position accounted for a large portion of the company's revenue. L.E.'s only problem, initially, in Missouri, was that he didn't realize he needed to wear wool socks instead of silk ones, to keep his feet warm. But, he soon learned.

L.E. was then returned to San Antonio, Texas, in 1975 as an equipment chief, in the special services district. He managed an outside plant organization, which had the responsibilities of overseeing Federal Aviation Administration (FAA) services, and other data services; that extended through out America into various foreign countries. Upon his arrival back in San Antonio he went to St. Mary's to talk with Brother Kohennan, Dean of the School of Business. He wanted the dean to know that he had achieved management for a major company, as a black man. The dean would have been so proud. However, it was found out that Dean Kohennan had passed away.

L.E. was known as a disciplined man by whites and blacks. He's had several negative encounters through the years by whites in management or that he supervised, but each time L.E. stood his ground. The majority knew where the line was and dared not cross it. L.E. retired from the phone company, in December of 1986, after thirty years of a successful career in helping others, and seeing the company become one of the best employers at offering equal opportunity to all segments of the San Antonio community. As a second level manager, he had under his control, at one time, fifty-one technicians, and ten management employees. His organization was responsible for installing and maintaining the 911 Emergency service for the city of San Antonio. He also was responsible for building the largest special services work center, in the history of Southwestern Bell. At that time it was located at 107 W. Nakoma, but is now occupied by A.T. & T company. L.E. selected the sight, along with another second level manager, and laid out the floor plans for his operating forces. What an amazing transformation, from janitor to second-level management. He was a competent, valued, and respected employee.

## THE STRUGGLE

HE FOUGHT IN THE BATTLE
FOR THE CAUSE OF CIVIL RIGHTS
GOD IS GOOD, ALL THE TIME!
THE STRUGGLE WAS NEARING AN END
THE BATTLE TO ELEVATE MINORITIES
IN THE WORK PLACE WAS WON,
BUT THE SPIRITUAL STRUGGLE WAS
STILL THERE AND
BEGAN TO TAKE
DOMINANCE IN HIS LIFE.

## SHARON BENNETT-WILLIAMS

# CHAPTER XI

During the families years in Corpus Christi, they became involved in their community, joining the St. Matthew Missionary Baptist Church, where Rev. Elliot Grant was the pastor. L.E. was placed on the deacon board, and Essie was an usher. The children participated in children's church, which they loved, except for one thing, Mrs. Fuquar, who was a middle aged woman of average height, skinny, and thick bifocals. But, she was also cock-eyed. One eye went left and the other one went right, so whenever she instructed or disciplined a child verbally, they became confused.

Once she had fussed at Louis, and Sharon said, "Are you talking to me?"

Mrs. Fuquar would say, "Was I looking at you, I wasn't talking to you."

Sharon would retort, "I don't know, you were looking at me."

"Looking at you, how could I have been looking at you, when I'm fussing at him," Mrs. Fuquar replied."

Louis came to his sisters defense, pointing his finger at Mrs. Fuquar with a serious look on his face and said, "With that eye, how are we suppose to know who you're looking at?"

The group of kids started to laugh. "Shut up that nonsense and get back to practicing your kazoo's," she'd shout.

The experiences at the church were memorable for the family. The church had undertaken the building of new low income apartments financed by the Federal Government. L.E. served as chairman of the Advisory Committee. They would be working closely with a Mr. Harris, a representative of the government out of San Antonio. L.E. assisted with bringing the project through its formative stage, and was looking forward to seeing to its conclusion, but a promotion and relocation back to San Antonio wouldn't allow that completion. Participation in this project would bring to remembrance the time he and Essie tried varied business ventures to earn extra income.

L.E. and Essie worked nights cleaning a bank building for a while, but that didn't pan out. On one occasion L.E. along with several other young men, one being Mr. Sam Johnson, a local barber, established a small business club. Their goal was to start the business by renting space to sell department store type merchandise. The market seemed ripe, for this type of undertaking, and they were ready to give it an earnest try, but it didn't prosper. The next go at business was to open a night club, on Greenwood street. People were always saying there was no place really nice to go except down on the "Cuts". The Cuts was an area off Leopard Street where black businesses were located. Saint Matthew and Mom's cafÈ were in walking distance. There were one and two-story run down buildings, with several night clubs, gambling joints, liquor stores, and companionship of the opposite sex, if one so desired. During the day it looked baron and desolate. But at night, it came alive and you could get all the action you were looking for. When you wanted to shake your booty and have a funky good time, or for home cooking of smothered steak with onions, rice, and gravy, you'd go to the Cuts. To hear the juke box blaring with songs by B.B. King, "Sweet Sixteen", or the Temptations singing, "I've got Sunshine", or Sam Cooke, "I Was Born By the River".

If you were so inclined, one could do some gambling and raise a little hell; or take a chance on losing your life. One could get a good dose of black culture on the Cuts. You had to think fast, and move twice as fast, and if you stayed too long in one place, someone just might call the undertaker. The Cuts was the place where you wore the latest fashions, and your best cologne. L.E. and Essie called their club the "Tropics", but it wasn't what you would call a barn burner. One Saturday, shortly after twelve noon, L.E. was there by himself. A gentleman, perhaps, in his early forties, came in and walked up to the bar, where L.E. was seated.

L.E. spoke to the man saying, "Afternoon, how are you?"

The gentleman replied, "I'm doing just fine, how about yourself?"

"Not too bad. What can I get you?", stated L.E.

The gentleman proceeded to ask for some information. Such as where he can find some gambling? L.E. didn't really know, but suspected that activity could be found down on the "Cuts". The gentleman then inquired as to where he could find a girl? Again, L.E. didn't know, but recommended the "Cuts".

Finally, the gentleman said, "You know, when I walked in here and looked at you, I could tell right away that this is not the place for you to be. Anybody, whose in this type of business would know the answer to those questions. But you don't, and that's because you don't care about those things. They are not of interest to you. I want to give you some good advice. Go back to church, where you belong! This is not your type of business. You will never be happy doing this type of thing." The gentleman then bided L.E. a good-day, got off the bar stool, and made his way through the front door.

Names were never exchanged, but L.E. knew the gentleman was right. He knew that the place for him was in church. Being anywhere else, L.E. felt like a fish out of water. He told Essie about the encounter, and shortly thereafter, they agreed to close the "Tropics", and get back to what they knew best, serving the Lord.

Well, L.E. participated in church as a deacon, Sunday school teacher, singer in the male chorus, and church business administrator, but preaching was not what he wanted. Reverend Grant, Reverend Langham, and Reverend Graham would all tell him, in their own way, that he had a call to acknowledge. Rev. Grant had to leave town on a family emergency and asked that L.E. bring the lesson for Sunday's service. L.E. finally agreed, but would not stand behind the pulpit. Instead, he stood below the staging, in front of the congregation, and delivered the lesson. However, this little gesture didn't force him to acknowledge the call.

It was February 6, 1988, L.E. and Ray had been at Martha's house, in San Antonio, visiting. Having their usual Saturday drinks and parlay. It was a beautiful sunny day, not a cloud in the sky. L.E. started home, between noon and one p.m., riding down highway 35, for no particular reason, he began to cry uncontrollably. He didn't understand what was happening until he reached home. L.E. could not stop crying until he confessed that he'd been called to preach. God had imposed his will upon him, without saying a word. The Lord never allowed him to get away. He got by for awhile, but not away. When L.E. began to outwardly acknowledge his call to others, it was as though a tremendous load had been lifted from his shoulders. It had been a breath of freedom, that he enjoys, even today. Perhaps, the Apostle Paul felt a breath of freedom, when he was knocked from his beast while on his way to persecute the Christians? You will never know the joys that life has in store, until you yield to God, and do his will. It's precious.

Upon reflection, L.E. could not help but think of how as a child of our Heavenly Father, we tend not to listen, and we want to do as we please, thinking we know it all.

His brother Lloyd became that way once. Lloyd felt that as a teenager he was grown, and he could do as he pleased. He was six feet, but he wasn't grown and he got on the wrong side of Anice with his temperament and attitude. The two exchanged words and she told Lloyd that if he couldn't obey her, then it would be best for him to get his own place, then he could do whatever he wanted. But, as long as he lived under her roof, he'll do as he's told. Lloyd immediately went to pack his bag, and bid his younger brothers good-bye. Floyd, Ray, and L.E. sat on the front porch, as they watched Lloyd amble down the gravel road. Finally, Lloyd stopped and sat in a culvert under a bridge. After a while, Floyd jumped up and went into the house. Momma, I think Blow wants to come back home. Can we go tell him to come back, Floyd asked?

"No, said Anice. I didn't ask him to leave, and I'm not asking him to come back. Blow made the decision to leave, now let him make the decision to come back on his own. He doesn't need any help to make up his mind about that." After about another hour, Blow got up and started back toward the house. Floyd, Ray, and L.E. hollered, "Momma, Blow is comming back home." When Anice heard Blow's feet hit the porch, she met him at the door.

"Where are you going, Blow?"

"I'm coming home, Momma."

Like a midget shaking her finger at a giant, Anice said, "Let me tell you something mister, I'm in charge at this house, and if you are going to stay here, you'd better learn that you are going to follow my rules and regulations, or else find another place to live. Do you understand me?"

Lloyd (Blow) said, "Yes, Mame, I understand."

Anice headed back to the kitchen talking steadily. "I don't ever want you thinking that you are going to tell me how you going to act around here. I'm the person who says what goes on around here and not you."

The world belongs to our Heavenly Father, and we best learn how to live by his rules and regulations, as governed by the Holy Spirit. We ,constantly, go around telling him what we will or will not do, and ignoring his wishes for our lives. Let's get it straight, we are not really in charge.

## BIBLICAL THOUGHT

As the people of Israel, we tend to focus on material gains and complain about what we don't have. Instead of being thankful, we lust for other objects. Don't take your blessings for granted! Depend and lean on the Lord. He's preparing you for something better transition.
Lusting leads to greed. Once we acquire it, we're left empty, incomplete, and with a dead soul.

We're happy when we receive blessings, but
days to weeks later, we complain about it.

Remember where God has brought you from. God still meets
your needs of food, shelter, clothing, and health. Remember to always
give thanks for your situation in life.

# CHAPTER XII

Well, the night finally arrived, February 21, 1988, and L.E. thought he would be real nervous. Since he'd spent so much time running from what God had called him to do, he feared this event so much. He recalled the night of high school graduation when he attempted to sing, and how his voice had cracked. Of late, he had sung in the male chorus and led songs, as well, with little or no difficulty. He loved the many capacities at which he served. But, preaching was a horse of a different color. He remembered the frightening revelation that occurred to him as a child. How he froze before a congregation of unknown people, how embarrassing. Yet, he didn't feel any butterflies. Maybe, it was going to come crashing down on him, when he walked up to the pulpit. L.E. sat in the back office and began his meditation, awaiting the notice for him to appear. He could hear the Mt. Calvary choir humming. This was a really great singing congregation, with wonderful leads. Then came a knock on the door, and a voice said the choir was doing their last number.

L.E. finished his preparations, and headed for the rostrum. The walk seemed like an eternity, but soon he opened the door to the sanctuary. The house was packed, and the other ministers stood as L.E. ascended the steps. Pastor Graham pointed to the seat L.E. was to take, but L.E. was looking for only one face, and that was Essie Lee's. When he spotted her, she smiled at him, and with that encouragement everything seemed right with the world. After preliminaries and the introduction by Pastor Graham, L.E. stepped to the pulpit, to suddenly feel an immense calm over him. It was as though he'd been doing this for years, no fear and no nervousness.

The topic was "A prisoner wrapped up in the love of the Lord" 2Timothy 1:1-4. The spirit of God held him up, and has continued to hold him up ever since. L.E. would later speak with Sister Langham, who had sent for him while Rev. Langham was ill. However, the good Reverend would pass before seeing him. He told Sister Langham to be sure to tell L.E. that if he had not started preaching, then to stop playing with God. He must go on and do what he knows God has called him to do. L.E. was now exercising his gift, he just wished Rev. Langham had lived to see it for himself.

L.E. feels that the big struggle at the onset of becoming a preacher was living the life. Others must be convinced that you have changed from what you once were, to what God has called you to be. Your life must be an example and light to others, not a stumbling block. People are not blind and naive, especially, your own family. If you are not living the life of a saved solider, it will be reflected to your family and the world. In which case they will have little respect for what you say from the pulpit. A preacher is tested at every turn. People need to know that your faith is genuine. Making up your mind is not the sole issue, it's sticking to your guns; because Satan is going to try real hard to make you think that you've made a mistake in choosing this life.

Having been a manager with Southwestern Bell, gave L.E. a lot of insight on handling people, from the managerial point of view. But, pastoring a congregation, is another breed of animal. With the phone company, people came to work, knowing that they have a certain schedule to meet, and that they are held accountable. Failing to meet those standards would mean certain sanctions, which may effect their paychecks. Not so with a church. Church people are free moral agents, and if they decided to sleep in on Sunday morning, for whatever reason, it is their prerogative. All a pastor can do is fill the position with another available soul, or do it himself. There is no such thing as calling them, and telling them they had better come to church in half an hour, or else. So, what threat do you use on a Sunday school teacher, deacon, usher, or choir member? All you can do is empathize with them, and hope that they are serious enough about their chosen work in the church to be committed to the job from then on.

During this period, L.E. was a first line supervisor on the 17c Testboard and Circuit Order Group, in San Antonio. There was this one individual who decided that since he was a brother, that he didn't have to be on time for work. L.E. had not been long on this supervisory job, when this person tried to test L.E. The first two times, nothing was said. But, when this man continued, and showed up late on the third morning, L.E. waited for him at the door. L.E. asked him If he was having a problem getting to work on time, and was there something he could do to help? The man stated that he didn't see any big problem with being late sometimes, and no reason to get bent out of shape. L.E. explained that he had a responsibility to be on time for work, and if he had difficulty reporting at 8:00a.m., then he could change him to a shift that would suit him best. L.E. further expressed that the very next time the man walked into the door after 8:00 a.m., and was shooting the breeze in the hallway before beginning work, that his shift would be changed. From that day forward, the man was never late again. You can not do this with a church worker, they would simply say, give the job to someone else, after all, they aren't paid.

With church work, you have to learn how to smooth ruffled feathers, and never forget to hand out the recognition and praise in ample quantity. So, when you speak to someone that is a fine worker in the church, remember, they are volunteers, serving the Lord, working out their salvation in fear and in trembling. Their pay day is not here on earth, it resides in a place called Heaven. You have to be thankful for the faithful few. Dedicated church workers are precious. They can do so much to help make or break a program. Please, don't get on the wrong side of one of your faithful workers, because if they leave service, it may be a long cold winter before you get an adequate replacement. However, at the same time, you must follow God's program, and do the right thing, so it's a delicate balance.

On the job, people like to hear praise as well, but they wait for their annual appraisal, to find out just how well the supervisor thinks they are doing. In the church, the Pastor has to continuously pat some workers on the back, to let them know then and there, that their efforts are really appreciated. Heaven forbid, you start thanking folks and leave someone out. That's major trouble. Christians should be doing works, because it's what God expects, not to get a pat on the back. A mature Christian realizes their glory is in the Lord, and could care less if they get worldly praise. They'll say thank you, that's nice, but won't scorn others if their name wasn't mentioned. These are even more rare and precious.

The average Baptist Pastor dresses just like the average man on the street. L.E. did not walk the streets in the robe, that he preaches in. He dresses in a suit and tie when out and about taking care of business. So, it is not unusual for someone on occasion to use fowl language or flirt. Once they are close enough to introduce themselves, it's amazing how the conversation changes, and their interest, when they find out you're a preacher. The life of a called man of God is not an easy road to travel, because temptation comes in so many beautiful packages, and it takes a made up mind, to remember what side your bread is buttered on. Ministers are not a perfect people, only God, whom they represent, is perfect. However, they are to live by and be led by the Holy Spirit, and are expected to conduct themselves in such a manner that will reflect Godliness.

The pleasure of female company is always appealing. Women are some of the most beautiful creatures that God placed on this green earth. If God has blessed a man with normal hormones, it is a difficult problem not to notice a beautiful woman. They are everywhere, and once you become a preacher, it seems as though there are more of them.

There are three Godly relationships in the Bible. Brother to sister, man to wife, and man to God. When you are led by the spirit, and you look at another woman, you should see her as your Christian sister. You don't think ungodly thoughts of your sister or brother. Even the thought is sin, and with the Holy Spirit, this temptation should not be such a struggle. However, with many, it is. God placed within man a natural proclivity, to reach out to the feminine gender. He also set a certain criteria by which it is to take place. Once married, a man is to cleave to his wife, their soul becomes one. This is the point procreation is to take place, and the married couple receives the best gift of all from God-the gift of sex. You are not supposed to desire another, and your hormones are to only be activated for her, if your walk in the spirit is true.

A pastor can not expect to shepard a flock and have a prospering church, if he himself is not leading his life as God intended. A minister should not be a stumbling block for his congregation, and if he falls in this way, he must confess it and not repeat the act. God still expects mankind to keep His house in order, in spite of what Satan may throw your way. Also, a pastor can not expect his church home to be in order, if his own home is not in order. Make no mistake about it, it is definitely an uphill journey, every step of the way.

## DON'T FORGET IT, OR ELSE YOU'LL REPEAT IT

KNOW YOUR HISTORY AND FROM WHENCE YOU CAME
DON'T FORGET IT, OR ELSE YOU'LL REPEAT IT

LIFE IS GOOD, AND GODS BLESSINGS GREAT
BUT, IS THE STRUGGLE OVER?
DON'T FORGET, OR ELSE YOU'LL REPEAT IT

DO YOU SMILE IN SOMEONE'S FACE,
AND SPITE THEM BEHIND THEIR BACK
DO YOU SPURN YOUR CHILD BECAUSE THEY'RE
CLOSE TO SOMEONE OF A DIFFERENT RACE
AN IGNORANT RACIST IS NOT ALWAYS WHITE
AND A DUMB NIGGA IS NOT ALWAYS BLACK
DON'T FORGET IT, OR ELSE YOU'LL REPEAT IT

WE STILL HAVE A LONG WAY TO GO
TO GET A LEVEL PLAYING FIELD
DON'T FORGET IT, OR ELSE YOU'LL REPEAT IT

MANY HAVE DIED FOR THE CAUSE OF CIVIL RIGHTS
BLACKS, JEWS, AND WHITES
OUR HISTORIES ARE RICH AND MUST STAY ALIVE
DON'T FORGET IT, OR ELSE YOU'LL
REPEAT IT

**SHARON BENNETT-WILLIAMS**

# CHAPTER XIII

L. E. was often called upon to visit the sick. On one particular
morning the doorbell rang. It was Mrs. Ned Cox, a neighbor.
She asked L.E. if he could go and counsel with her husband,
because Ned wished to speak with him. L.E. arrived one afternoon
to find Ned deathly ill with cancer. All therapies had been tried, and
he was given a short time to live. L.E. and Ned talked, he prayed with
Ned, and then he left. As L.E. exited the front door, he stopped dead
in his tracks, overcome with emotion. He never knew. Could he had
been so consumed with his civil rights efforts that he was oblivious
to the feelings of some of his own people?

Ned had also been a phone company employee, who acquired
management sometime after L.E. He told L.E. that some blacks
were jealous and extremely envious of the work he had done to
promote blacks. Many did not appreciate his efforts. They wanted
the pot stirred, but not by some young Johnny come lately. However,
if things were to go wrong, L.E. would have had to take the fall.

Ned then said, "Thank you, I just have to tell you this before I
die. I appreciate all that you've done. You've helped a lot of people
who were too afraid to do it for themselves."

L.E. was filled with emotions of anger as he drove home. A heart
felt thank you, from a non-union member. L.E. reflected on the long
hard fight, the many days and nights away from his family. Driving
the lonely roads from city to city, to encourage union members
to want a better life; now he found that some were jealous and

others were grateful for the change, but not enough to thank him for it. Only Carl Ray Randle had acknowledged his efforts during that period. L.E. worked his tail off, neglecting his family, and he continues to do so with the same fervor as a pastor.

Though people are different, they are also the same. You visit their sick, marry their relatives, bury their dead, help them through their problems, and still they will turn on you when opportunity presents itself. But, then you don't do it to receive glory from man, you do it for the glory of God; and because it's the right thing to do. That's what leadership is all about. This brings to mind when L.E. was at the phone companies general headquarters, in St. Louis, MO, for a "skip-level" meeting with other young company managers. This meeting was designed to give the younger managers a chance to speak with upper level management and gain insight on company policy and opportunities for advancement. The meeting was presided over by Mr. Randy Barron, the Vice President. The tables were set in a u formation, with Mr. Barron sitting up front at the opening of the u.

There was a young white male manager, sitting next to L.E., a second level manager, who raised his hand for a question on promotions. This young man felt that white males were being skipped over, in favor of giving promotions to others who may be less qualified, thus, somewhat minimizing the opportunities for white males. Mr. Barron began his answer saying that he remembered when he was a young district manager back in Oklahoma. Sitting behind his desk and seeing a panoramic view of opportunities for promotions. L.E. then raised his hand to be acknowledged.

Stating, "Mr. Barron, I think the company is to be congratulated for opening the window of opportunity to all of her employees. Because, when you were sitting at your desk in Oklahoma looking at that panoramic view, the view for me and these women here were just like this, holding his clinched fist up to his eye, we didn't have any. If this young man sitting here next to me has so many qualifications, maybe he should be sitting where you are, instead of being over here by me."

Mr. Barron replied in agreement. The company is making great progress in giving all employees opportunities to advance. Southwestern Bell and A.T. & T had become a giant in the field of communications, offering a chance for all of the citizens that she serves. Things change and yet, they stay the same.

L.E. was ordained March 20, 1988 by his father in the ministry, Rev. C.M. Graham. He served as an associate pastor until he was called as pastor, February 13, 1989, of the Galilee Missionary Baptist Church in San Antonio, Texas. Everything seemed to be happening so fast. The whole family moved membership in support of L.E., and he was so proud of them all. Louis was still away serving in the Air Force, but would be there on every leave. Sharon was working at USAA (United Services Automobile Association), and putting herself through school for a second degree, this one in nursing, as well as being a single mom. Lisa was in California trying to spread her wings of independence, and working. Kenneth was working in carpentry, at the time. It was hard work getting things organized. Sharon and Kenneth sang in the choir, as well as, taught Sunday school. The building was old and in need of many repairs. Fundraisers and various projects were underway to make improvements.

As the pastor of Galilee, L.E. became involved with the Westend Neighborhood Association, working on neighborhood improvements on the west side of San Antonio. L.E. became chairman of the housing committee, and worked closely with councilwoman Maria Berriozabal, and later councilman Roger Flores. L.E. was instrumental in obtaining street improvements, and having approximately nineteen new low income houses built in the area. He helped with the implementation of the Micklejohn Revitalization Plan, which was designed to bring about the clearance of blight from the area. It wasn't ever long before L.E. was asked to participate in, or lead an endeavor. He has always been industrious and productive. This trait he inherited from his parents Anice and Dan. He was not one to sit long in a spot, doing absolutely nothing. L.E. has been a consistent force for a change. Efforts were underway, to have a senior citizens complex built.

Meanwhile, continued progress had been made in street and drainage improvements, as well as, removing some of the dilapidated vacant buildings from the general area. This made the area more conducive to attracting new families. All would seem to be going smoothly.

Except for Webb, L.E. had lived to see all of his brothers pass away. Each one caused an intense pain and took a part of L.E. with them. But, nothing could rival the anguish he felt on the night of July 25, 1991. The family's walls would come tumbling down with devastation. It was just a few minutes after midnight, when the phone rang. It was a call from a Houston funeral home director. After confirming that he was speaking to the correct party, he informed the Bennett's that their son, Kenneth, was dead. The body would be released to his funeral home, after autopsy completion. The police didn't have the decency to call first.

Kenneth always seemed so restless and unfulfilled. He always had a wild hair and was impatient with school. Possibly, this was one factor that pushed him into the dark life. Kenneth was highly intelligent and tried many things in life. He had worked for Frito-Lay, and Boeing, as a machinist. He attended the Hallmark School of Aviation, where he made A's and was on the honor roll. He had been tested to have an IQ of 160, but he was impatient with school. He even tried his hand at music promotions and parties. Kenneth was a handsome young man, who was extremely friendly and always well dressed. He worked out and lifted weights daily, and added wheat germ to his foods. Yet, his personality was that of a follower, instead of a leader. He always desired fame and fortune, and didn't have the patience to work a regular job to earn a good living, that either of those companies could have afforded him. The darkened lure of the streets was strong, and they beckoned him, again and again. Kenneth never stole from his parents, and it grieved him to think that he was a disappointment or a source of embarrassment for his family. He put himself in a position that took his life, so he couldn't return home.

He had spent the day in San Antonio with his nephew Jerrick, Sharon's son. They worked, drank sodas, and talked. He returned

Jerrick home, and then headed to see his brother Louis in Austin, that same evening, so they could talk over old times. He told Louis he was going to Houston to see a relative, a place where his life had once been threatened, if he were ever seen again. Just after he dropped off Jerrick, he had met an acquaintance, and the two of them robbed a drug dealer in San Antonio. This sealed his inability to return to San Antonio. Kenneth made some connections in Houston, and then attended a party that night where three men tried to rob him and a fight ensued. Kenneth was strong and a good boxer. He took a knife from one, stabbing the attacker with it in the knee. He was able to get out of the house, but not before he was stabbed with a needle of toxic drugs, on his right flank, between the $3^{rd}$ and $4^{th}$ ribs. There was one thing he always feared in life, and that was needles. The marks were still on his shirt and undershirt. Kenneth ran through the streets screaming for someone to call the police and an ambulance. But, the running only made the drug work faster. He collapsed in an old mans arms, while holding a brick. The gentleman called 911, and then returned to hold Kenneth safely in his arms, until the police and ambulance arrived. We are forever indebted to this mans kindness.

Sharon always had sort of a sixth sense. As a child she frequently spoke to a friend, she called ghosty. She described him as a really big tall man, whose head passed the doorway, and who was friendly and gentle.

The night of her brothers death, she'd been out with a friend, and decided to stay over, since it was closer to school. She'd had an urge to talk with her brother all evening. But never got a response when she called him. Just before midnight, she abruptly awoke with the feeling that her heart had stopped. Now, she was desperate to speak with Kenneth. Still no answer at his apartment. The following morning, Essie called Sharon, asking her to come home before going to school. Sharon told Essie that would be the opposite direction, and why couldn't it wait until after class? Essie retorted, that she needed to talk to Sharon in person. Sharon hung up the phone, and told her friend that her premonition had been realized, her brother was dead. He achieved self-destruction.

This loss was unbelievable to the Bennett family, as well as, unbearable. A parent never expects to outlive their child. That's just not the natural order of things. How can you endure after the loss of a child? The church was packed with standing room only, and more people were standing outside. Though, it was a horrible loss, the Bennett's were not unique in their experience. Unfortunately, death is a part of everyday life, and the heartache is felt over and over. No matter what anyone says, you never get over it, you only learn to bear a vague resemblance of living with it.

## MY SWEET CHILD

OH, MY SWEET DEAR CHILD,
THE ONE I HELPED RAISE INTO A MAN,
THE ONE I WATCHED AS HE PLAYED BALL,
DID HIS HOMEWORK, OR JUST
PLAYED WITH HIS SIBLINGS.

THE DAY I SAW YOU WAS FILLED
WITH IMMENSE JOY AND HAPPINESS,
BUT, THE DAY I LOST YOU WAS OVERCOME
WITH SADNESS AND PAIN.

THE YOUNG BOY WHOSE EYES GLOWED WITH PROMISE
ARE NOW EXTINGUISHED IN DEATH.
THE ONE I GAVE TOUGH LOVE TO,
AND HELD HIGH HOPES FOR.

THAT SMILED, EAGER TO PLEASE HIS FATHER,
AND HIS MOTHER.
HIS BRILLIANT LIGHT IS NOW, NO MORE.

SLEEP SWEET CHILD SLEEP,
YOUR ANGUISH IS OVER,

## AND WE ALL MISS YOU DEARLY. THE MOMENT IS IMPATIENTLY AWAITED, WHEN WE SHALL ALL MEET AGAIN.

### SHARON BENNETT-WILLIAMS (2000)

The family continued to plug away with their daily lives. L.E. dug himself deeper into his work as pastor, and in the community. He served as the secretary of the Guadalupe District Missionary Baptist Association and College, INC., and as Chairman of the Board of the Directors. The Directors also have oversight responsibility for the Guadalupe Theological College. L.E. has also served as treasurer of the WestSide Ministerial Alliance of San Antonio, as well as vice-president and president. He served as president of the Alamo City Lions Club, and a member of the Golden Mile Optimist Club. He was a board member for the Bexar County Opportunities Industrialization Center of America (B.C.O.I.C.A.) and the San Antonio Local Development Company Trustees, and a member of the Baptist Ministers Union of San Antonio and vicinity.

On October 1997 Galilee moved into its new $100,000 sanctuary, using the old structure as a fellowship hall. It's known as the little church, with a big heart. L.E. received his Bachelor of Theology in 1992, and his Master of Theology in 1994, from the Guadalupe Theological College. He was awarded a Doctor of Divinity from Guadalupe in 1997.

Life is a never ending struggle, until you die. A productive life is one where you help others, and not just yourself. Being a pastor means being a servant to God by serving man. This is what L.E. has done, and is still doing. This man has had a fruitful life, enjoying its harvest, as well as suffering its agony.

> May God bless and keep you is the family's prayer!
> Live each day to its fullest in good service,
> because tomorrow is not promised to you.

# AFTERWARD

L.E. Bennett's life of civil rights activities was one illuminated. There were many who answered the call to struggle in the battle of equal opportunities for blacks, and all minorities. It took thousands to make this change in America and a few to lead the fight, yet, we have the same struggle that existed in Gettysburg. This, our land of opportunity and land of diversity.

Conditions have improved for minorities in America, but don't make the mistake of believing the war is over. It has merely been subdued, because racism still rages in America. Racism against the color of your skin, your sexual preferences, the car you drive, the house you live in, the religion you worship, the company you keep, the way you wear your hair, or the color of your eyes. Racism against just being different.

Praises to those who value and appreciate the differences within the human race. They have seen the light. Empathy to those who rather waste their energy hating instead of in a productive life. Remember, the only original inhabitants of America were the Indians. So, if anyone needs to go back somewhere, guess who it is.

### BECKON OF LIGHT

They were not there when your brow
was heavy with stress
When you contemplated which action to take,
a better way for us you wanted to make
How dare they over rehearse
Their lines of disdain, in this your hour of pain

Yes, made by God's Holy Hand
You are yet a man
For there's only one that was perfect,
did He send
For all the years you suffered and strived to make a way

Yet they contrive and down their noses lay

Look to the beckon of family
your light they've always been
look to our Lord and Savior
as he looked to his Father back then

Time will be hard and slow,
But just keep looking into that beckon of light,
Because in it God's mercy always flows

(By: Sharon Bennett-Williams/ Inspired by Rev. Jesse Jackson)

## ABOUT THE AUTHOR

Sharon Bennett-Williams is a professional nurse by craft, and a writer by soul. She was born and raised in San Antonio, Texas. She's written poems and short stories since her early teens. Three poems, and one short story have been published. She resides in the Atlanta area with her husband, Burnett M. Williams, and two children, Jerrick l. Bennett, a student of technical engineering at Devry; and Sharena l. Perkins, a pre-law student at Georgia State University. Meet L.E. Bennett is her first casually written biography.

## ABOUT GREATUNPUBLISHED.COM

greatunpublished.com is a website that exists to serve writers and readers, and remove some of the commercial barriers between them. When you purchase a greatunpublished.com title, whether you receive it in electronic form or in a paperback volume or as a signed copy of the author's manuscript, you can be assured that the author is receiving a majority of the post-production revenue. Writers who join greatunpublished.com support the site and its marketing efforts with a per-title fee, and a portion of the site's share of profits are channeled into literacy programs.

So by purchasing this title from greatunpublished.com, you are helping to revolutionize the publishing industry for the benefit of writers and readers.
And for this we thank you.